ITIL 4 Foundation

Exam Insights:

Q & A with Explanations

SUJAN

ITIL 4 Foundation

Exam Insights: Q & A with Explanations

FIRST EDITION. September 10th, 2024.

COPYRIGHT © 2024 SUJAN.

Written by SUJAN

CONTENTS

Examination Format

- 40 questions
- Multiple choice
- 26 out of 40 marks required to pass (65%)
- 60 minutes
- Closed book.

INTRODUCTION :

Welcome to "ITIL 4 Foundation Exam Insights: Q & A with Explanations." This essential guide is designed to be your trusted ally on the journey to mastering the ITIL 4 Foundation certification. This book serves as a comprehensive resource for practice, featuring a robust collection of questions, detailed answers, and thorough explanations to help you succeed in your exam.

Tailored for both newcomers to IT service management and seasoned professionals looking to solidify their ITIL knowledge, "ITIL 4 Foundation Exam Insights" is an indispensable tool. It offers a range of practice questions that reflect the format and complexity of the actual ITIL 4 Foundation exam. Each question is accompanied by detailed explanations that not only clarify the correct answers but also deepen your understanding of key ITIL concepts and practices.

Whether you are preparing for the ITIL 4 Foundation exam or seeking to enhance your IT service management skills, this book provides a focused and effective approach to your study. With extensive practice opportunities and insightful explanations, "ITIL 4 Foundation Exam Insights" is designed to support your preparation and boost your confidence as you work toward achieving your certification goals.

PRACTICE TEST - 1

Question 1

What is the primary purpose of a Service Value Stream in ITIL 4?

A) To define the steps required to deliver a specific IT service

B) To identify the key stakeholders involved in a service

C) To map the flow of activities and processes that create value for customers

D) To measure the performance of individual IT teams

Answer: C) To map the flow of activities and processes that create value for customers

Explanation: A Service Value Stream is a series of connected activities and processes that create value for customers by providing a specific service. It helps organizations visualize and optimize the flow of work to deliver value to customers efficiently.

Question 2

Which of the following is a key benefit of designing and implementing Service Value Streams in ITIL 4?

A) Improved incident resolution times

B) Increased efficiency and reduced waste in service delivery

C) Enhanced customer satisfaction through personalized services

D) Better alignment of IT services with business strategy

Answer: B) Increased efficiency and reduced waste in service delivery

Explanation: Service Value Streams help organizations streamline their processes, eliminate unnecessary steps, and reduce waste, leading to increased efficiency and improved service delivery. By focusing on value creation, organizations can optimize their resources and improve overall performance.

Question 3

What is the role of the "Engage" stage in the ITIL 4 Service Value System?

A) To design and develop new services based on customer feedback

B) To build and test services to ensure they meet customer requirements

C) To understand customer needs and preferences to co-create value

D) To deliver and support services to customers

Answer: C) To understand customer needs and preferences to co-create value

Explanation: The "Engage" stage is the initial stage of the ITIL 4 Service Value System, where organizations work with customers to understand their needs, preferences, and expectations. This stage focuses on co-creating value by understanding customer requirements and involving them in the service design process.

Question 4

Which of the following ITIL 4 practices is responsible for ensuring that services are delivered and supported in accordance with agreed-upon service level agreements (SLAs)?

A) Continual Improvement and Feedback

B) Service Request Management

C) Service Level Management

D) Incident Management

Answer: C) Service Level Management

Explanation: Service Level Management is the ITIL 4 practice responsible for ensuring that services are delivered and supported in accordance with agreed-upon SLAs. This practice focuses on managing service levels, negotiating SLAs with customers, and monitoring service performance to ensure that agreed-upon levels are met.

Question 5

What is the primary goal of the "Design and Transition" stage in a Service Value Stream?

A) To deliver and support services to customers

B) To understand customer needs and preferences

C) To create and transition new or changed services into production

D) To continuously improve and refine services

Answer: C) To create and transition new or changed services into production

Explanation: The "Design and Transition" stage is a critical part of a Service Value Stream, where new or changed services are designed, built, and transitioned into production. This stage ensures that services are properly designed, tested, and deployed to meet customer requirements.

Question 6

Which of the following is a key characteristic of a Service Value Stream in ITIL 4?

A) It focuses on a single IT service or process

B) It is linear and sequential, with no feedback loops

C) It is a series of connected activities that create value for customers

D) It is only applicable to new services, not existing ones

Answer: C) It is a series of connected activities that create value for customers

Explanation: A Service Value Stream is a series of connected activities and processes that create value for customers by providing a specific service. It is a holistic approach that considers the entire flow of work, from demand to delivery, to ensure that value is created for customers.

Question 7

What is the purpose of the "Obtain/Build" activity in a Service Value Stream?

A) To deliver and support services to customers

B) To design and develop new services

C) To procure or develop the necessary components and assets required to deliver a service

D) To test and validate services before deployment

Answer: C) To procure or develop the necessary components and assets required to deliver a service

Explanation: The "Obtain/Build" activity in a Service Value Stream is responsible for procuring or developing the necessary components and assets required to deliver a service. This includes acquiring goods, services, knowledge, and resources needed to create and deliver value to customers.

Question 8

Which of the following is a benefit of using Service Value Streams to manage IT services?

A) Improved incident resolution times only

B) Increased efficiency and reduced waste in service delivery

C) Enhanced customer satisfaction through personalized services only

D) Better alignment of IT services with business strategy only

Answer: B) Increased efficiency and reduced waste in service delivery

Explanation: Service Value Streams help organizations streamline their processes, eliminate unnecessary steps, and reduce waste, leading to increased efficiency and improved service delivery. By focusing on value creation, organizations can optimize their resources and improve overall performance. This benefit is a key outcome of implementing Service Value Streams in ITIL 4.

Question 9

Which ITIL 4 practice is responsible for ensuring that services are aligned with business objectives and are delivered to meet agreed-upon service level agreements (SLAs)?

A) Service Desk

B) Service Level Management

C) Continual Improvement and Feedback

D) IT Asset Management

Answer: B) Service Level Management

Explanation: Service Level Management is the ITIL 4 practice responsible for ensuring that services are aligned with business objectives and are delivered to meet agreed-upon SLAs. This practice focuses on managing service levels, negotiating SLAs with customers, and monitoring service performance to ensure that agreed-upon levels are met.

Question 10

What is the primary goal of the "Continual Improvement and Feedback" practice in ITIL 4?

A) To identify and manage risks associated with IT services

B) To ensure that IT services are delivered in accordance with agreed-upon SLAs

C) To continually improve and refine IT services based on feedback and performance data

D) To manage and control IT assets throughout their lifecycle

Answer: C) To continually improve and refine IT services based on feedback and performance data

Explanation: The "Continual Improvement and Feedback" practice in ITIL 4 focuses on continually improving and refining IT services based on feedback and performance data. This practice ensures that IT services are aligned with changing business needs and that opportunities for improvement are identified and addressed.

Question 11

What is the purpose of the "Request Fulfillment" activity in a Service Value Stream?

A) To design and develop new services

B) To procure or develop the necessary components and assets required to deliver a service

C) To deliver and support services to customers in response to their requests

D) To continually improve and refine services based on feedback and performance data

Answer: C) To deliver and support services to customers in response to their requests

Explanation: The "Request Fulfillment" activity in a Service Value Stream is responsible for delivering and supporting services to customers in response to their requests. This activity ensures that customer requests are fulfilled efficiently and effectively, and that services are delivered to meet customer needs.

Question 12

Which of the following is a key benefit of using Service Value Streams to manage IT services?

A) Improved incident resolution times only

B) Increased efficiency and reduced waste in service delivery, leading to cost savings and improved customer satisfaction

C) Enhanced customer satisfaction through personalized services only

D) Better alignment of IT services with business strategy only

Answer: B) Increased efficiency and reduced waste in service delivery, leading to cost savings and improved customer satisfaction

Explanation: Service Value Streams help organizations streamline their processes, eliminate unnecessary steps, and reduce waste, leading to increased efficiency and improved service delivery. This results in cost savings and improved customer satisfaction, as services are delivered more effectively and efficiently.

QUESTION 13

What is the primary goal of the "Design for Experience" principle in Service Value Streams?

A) To ensure that services are designed to meet agreed-upon service level agreements (SLAs)

B) To design services that are easy to use, meet customer needs, and provide a positive experience

C) To ensure that services are designed with the necessary security and compliance controls

D) To design services that are aligned with business objectives and strategy

Answer: B) To design services that are easy to use, meet customer needs, and provide a positive experience

Explanation: The "Design for Experience" principle in Service Value Streams focuses on designing services that are easy to use, meet customer needs, and provide a positive experience. This principle ensures that services are designed with the customer in mind, taking into account their needs, preferences, and pain points.

Question 14

Which activity in a Service Value Stream is responsible for ensuring that services are delivered and supported in accordance with agreed-upon service level agreements (SLAs)?

A) Engage

B) Design and Transition

C) Obtain/Build

D) Deliver and Support

Answer: D) Deliver and Support

Explanation: The "Deliver and Support" activity in a Service Value Stream is responsible for ensuring that services are delivered and supported in accordance with agreed-upon SLAs. This activity focuses on delivering services to customers, ensuring that services are available and accessible, and providing ongoing support to ensure continued value creation.

Question 15

What is the purpose of the "Engage" activity in a Service Value Stream?

A) To design and develop new services based on customer feedback

B) To build and test services to ensure they meet customer requirements

C) To understand customer needs and preferences to co-create value

D) To deliver and support services to customers

Answer: C) To understand customer needs and preferences to co-create value

Explanation: The "Engage" activity in a Service Value Stream is the initial stage of the value stream, where organizations work with customers to understand their needs, preferences, and expectations. This activity focuses on co-creating value by understanding customer requirements and involving them in the service design process.

QUESTION 16

Which of the following is a key characteristic of a Service Value Stream in ITIL 4?

A) It is a linear and sequential process with no feedback loops

B) It is a series of connected activities that create value for customers

C) It is focused solely on delivering IT services, not business outcomes

D) It is only applicable to new services, not existing ones

Answer: B) It is a series of connected activities that create value for customers

Explanation: A Service Value Stream is a series of connected activities and processes that create value for customers by providing a specific service. It is a holistic approach that considers the entire flow of work, from demand to delivery, to ensure that value is created for customers. This characteristic is a key aspect of Service Value Streams in ITIL 4.

Question 17

Which stage of the ITIL Service Lifecycle is responsible for ensuring that services are delivered and supported according to agreed-upon service level agreements (SLAs)?

A) Service Strategy

B) Service Design

C) Service Transition

D) Service Operation

Answer: D) Service Operation

Explanation: The Service Operation stage of the ITIL Service Lifecycle is responsible for delivering and supporting services according to agreed-upon SLAs. This stage focuses on managing the day-to-day delivery of services, ensuring that services are available and accessible, and providing ongoing support to ensure continued value creation.

Question 18

What is the primary goal of the Service Strategy stage in the ITIL Service Lifecycle?

A) To design and develop new services based on customer feedback

B) To build and test services to ensure they meet customer requirements

C) To define the service portfolio and develop the service strategy

D) To deliver and support services to customers

Answer: C) To define the service portfolio and develop the service strategy

Explanation: The Service Strategy stage of the ITIL Service Lifecycle is responsible for defining the service portfolio and developing the service strategy. This stage focuses on understanding customer needs, defining service offerings, and developing a strategy to deliver and support services that meet customer requirements and business objectives.

Question 19

What is the definition of a "service" in the context of ITIL 4?

A) A technical solution or system used to support business processes

B) A means of delivering value to customers by facilitating outcomes they want to achieve

C) A business process or function that supports IT services

D) A technical support team that resolves incidents and requests

Answer: B) A means of delivering value to customers by facilitating outcomes they want to achieve

Explanation: In ITIL 4, a service is defined as a means of delivering value to customers by facilitating outcomes they want to achieve. This definition focuses on the customer perspective and the value that services provide to them.

Question 20

What is the term for the "ability of an organization to adapt to changing circumstances" in ITIL 4?

A) Resilience

B) Agility

C) Flexibility

D) Scalability

Answer: B) Agility

Explanation: In ITIL 4, agility refers to the ability of an organization to adapt to changing circumstances, such as shifts in customer needs or market conditions. This concept is important in IT service management, as organizations need to be able to respond quickly to changing requirements and deliver value to customers in a rapidly changing environment.

Question 21

Which process in the Service Transition stage of the ITIL Service Lifecycle is responsible for planning and coordinating the deployment of changes to IT services?

A) Change Management

B) Service Asset and Configuration Management

C) Release and Deployment Management

D) Service Validation and Testing

Answer: C) Release and Deployment Management

Explanation: Release and Deployment Management is the process responsible for planning and coordinating the deployment of changes to IT services. This process ensures that changes are properly planned, built, tested, and deployed to production, minimizing disruption to IT services.

Question 22

What is the primary goal of the Continual Service Improvement (CSI) stage in the ITIL Service Lifecycle?

A) To design and develop new IT services

B) To deliver and support IT services to customers

C) To continually improve the quality and value of IT services

D) To manage and control IT service assets and configurations

Answer: C) To continually improve the quality and value of IT services

Explanation: The primary goal of the Continual Service Improvement (CSI) stage is to continually improve the quality and value of IT services. This stage focuses on identifying opportunities for improvement, analyzing data, and implementing changes to improve IT services and processes.

Question 23

Which process in the Service Operation stage of the ITIL Service Lifecycle is responsible for managing the lifecycle of all service requests from users?

A) Incident Management

B) Request Fulfilment

C) Problem Management

D) Event Management

Answer: B) Request Fulfilment

Explanation: Request Fulfilment is the process responsible for managing the lifecycle of all service requests from users. This process ensures that service requests are properly logged, assessed, approved, and fulfilled, providing a seamless experience for users.

Question 24

What is the primary objective of the Service Design stage in the ITIL Service Lifecycle?

A) To deliver and support IT services to customers

B) To design and develop new IT services and processes

C) To continually improve the quality and value of IT services

D) To manage and control IT service assets and configurations

Answer: B) To design and develop new IT services and processes

Explanation: The primary objective of the Service Design stage is to design and develop new IT services and processes. This stage focuses on turning service strategies into tangible designs and plans, ensuring that IT services meet customer needs and business objectives.

Question 25

Which process in the Service Transition stage of the ITIL Service Lifecycle is responsible for ensuring that IT services are withdrawn or terminated in a planned and controlled manner?

A) Change Management

B) Service Asset and Configuration Management

C) Release and Deployment Management

D) Service Retirement Management

Answer: D) Service Retirement Management

Explanation: Service Retirement Management is the process responsible for ensuring that IT services are withdrawn or terminated in a planned and controlled manner. This process ensures that services are properly decommissioned, and resources are released, minimizing disruption to remaining IT services.

Question 26

Which stage in the ITIL Service Lifecycle is responsible for ensuring that IT services are delivered and supported according to agreed-upon service level agreements (SLAs)?

A) Service Strategy

B) Service Design

C) Service Transition

D) Service Operation

Answer: D) Service Operation

Explanation: The Service Operation stage is responsible for ensuring that IT services are delivered and supported according to agreed-upon SLAs. This stage focuses on managing the day-to-day delivery of services, ensuring that services are available and accessible, and providing ongoing support to ensure continued value creation.

Question 27

What is the primary goal of value co-creation in IT service management?

A) To deliver IT services that meet business requirements

B) To provide IT services at a lower cost

C) To create value for customers and stakeholders through collaborative relationships

D) To improve IT service quality and reduce incidents

Answer: C) To create value for customers and stakeholders through collaborative relationships

Explanation: Value co-creation is about creating value for customers and stakeholders through collaborative relationships. It involves working together with customers and stakeholders to understand their needs and preferences and to create services that meet those needs.

Question 28

Which of the following is a key aspect of value co-creation in IT service management?

A) Focusing solely on IT service quality and availability

B) Understanding customer needs and preferences through collaborative relationships

C) Providing standardized IT services to all customers

D) Measuring IT service value solely through financial metrics

Answer: B) Understanding customer needs and preferences through collaborative relationships

Explanation: Understanding customer needs and preferences through collaborative relationships is a key aspect of value co-creation. This involves working closely with customers and stakeholders to understand their needs, preferences, and expectations, and to create services that meet those needs.

Question 29

What is the primary purpose of a business architecture in the context of IT service management?

A) To design and deliver IT services that meet business requirements

B) To define the business strategy and direction

C) To understand the business structure, processes, and relationships

D) To manage and control IT service assets and configurations

Answer: C) To understand the business structure, processes, and relationships

Explanation: A business architecture is a representation of the business structure, processes, and relationships. Its primary purpose is to provide a clear understanding of the business, enabling IT to deliver services that meet business needs and support business objectives.

Question 30

Which of the following is a key component of a business architecture?

A) IT service portfolio

B) IT infrastructure and applications

C) Business capabilities and processes

D) IT service level agreements (SLAs)

Answer: C) Business capabilities and processes

Explanation: Business capabilities and processes are key components of a business architecture. They describe the business functions, processes, and activities that create value for customers and stakeholders. Understanding these components is essential for IT to deliver services that support business objectives.

Question 31

What is the primary goal of the Continual Improvement model in ITIL 4?

A) To identify and implement new IT services and processes

B) To measure and report on IT service performance

C) To identify and address areas for improvement in IT services and processes

D) To define and agree on IT service level agreements (SLAs)

Answer: C) To identify and address areas for improvement in IT services and processes

Explanation: The Continual Improvement model in ITIL 4 aims to identify and address areas for improvement in IT services and processes. This model provides a structured approach to identifying opportunities for improvement, analyzing data, and implementing changes to improve IT services and processes.

Question 32

Which of the following is a key activity in the Continual Improvement model?

A) Defining IT service level agreements (SLAs)

B) Conducting regular service reviews and assessments

C) Implementing new IT services and processes

D) Managing and controlling IT service assets and configurations

Answer: B) Conducting regular service reviews and assessments

Explanation: Conducting regular service reviews and assessments is a key activity in the Continual Improvement model. This involves regularly reviewing and assessing IT services and processes to identify areas for improvement, measure performance, and identify opportunities for improvement.

Question 33

Which technical management practice is responsible for ensuring that IT infrastructure and applications are properly configured and maintained?

A) Infrastructure and Platform Management

B) Software Development and Maintenance

C) Technical Service Management

D) IT Asset Management

Answer: A) Infrastructure and Platform Management

Explanation: Infrastructure and Platform Management is the technical management practice responsible for ensuring that IT infrastructure and applications are properly configured and maintained. This practice focuses on managing the technical components of IT services, including hardware, software, and networking.

Question 34

Which technical management practice is responsible for ensuring that IT services are designed and developed to meet business requirements?

A) Service Design

B) Software Development and Maintenance

C) Technical Service Management

D) IT Quality Management

Answer: B) Software Development and Maintenance

Explanation: Software Development and Maintenance is the technical management practice responsible for ensuring that IT services are designed and developed to meet business requirements. This practice focuses on designing, developing, testing, and maintaining software applications that support IT services.

Question 35

Which technical management practice is responsible for ensuring the smooth operation of IT services by monitoring and controlling IT infrastructure and applications?

A) IT Operations Management

B) Infrastructure and Platform Management

C) Technical Service Management

D) Event Management

Answer: A) IT Operations Management

Explanation: IT Operations Management is the technical management practice responsible for ensuring the smooth operation of IT services by monitoring and controlling IT infrastructure and applications. This practice focuses on managing the day-to-day operational activities of IT services.

Question 36

Which technical management practice is responsible for ensuring that IT services are secure and resilient against cyber threats and other disruptions?

A) Information Security Management

B) IT Asset Management

C) Technical Service Management

D) Risk Management

Answer: A) Information Security Management

Explanation: Information Security Management is the technical management practice responsible for ensuring that IT services are secure and resilient against cyber threats and other disruptions. This practice focuses on managing information security risks, implementing security controls, and ensuring compliance with security policies.

Question 37

Which service management practice is responsible for ensuring that IT services are delivered and supported in a way that meets the agreed-upon service level agreements (SLAs)?

A) Service Level Management

B) Service Desk

C) Service Request Management

D) Continual Service Improvement

Answer: A) Service Level Management

Explanation: Service Level Management is the service management practice responsible for ensuring that IT services are delivered and supported in a way that meets the agreed-upon SLAs. This practice focuses on managing service levels, negotiating SLAs, and monitoring service performance.

Question 38

Which service management practice is responsible for providing a single point of contact for users to request IT services and report incidents?

A) Service Desk

B) Service Request Management

C) Incident Management

D) Problem Management

Answer: A) Service Desk

Explanation: The Service Desk is the service management practice responsible for providing a single point of contact for users to request IT services and report incidents. This practice focuses on managing user interactions, resolving simple incidents, and escalating complex issues to other teams.

Question 39

Which service management practice is responsible for managing the lifecycle of all changes to IT services, including assessment, approval, and implementation?

A) Change Control

B) Change Management

C) Service Validation and Testing

D) Release and Deployment Management

Answer: B) Change Management

Explanation: Change Management is the service management practice responsible for managing the lifecycle of all changes to IT services, including assessment, approval, and implementation. This practice focuses on ensuring that changes are properly planned, implemented, and verified to minimize disruption to IT services.

Question 40

Which service management practice is responsible for identifying, assessing, and mitigating risks to IT services, including identifying potential causes of incidents and problems?

A) Risk Management

B) Problem Management

C) Incident Management

D) Continual Service Improvement

Answer: A) Risk Management

Explanation: Risk Management is the service management practice responsible for identifying, assessing, and mitigating risks to IT services, including identifying potential causes of incidents and problems. This practice focuses on ensuring that IT services are resilient and can withstand disruptions, and that risks are identified and mitigated proactively.

PRACTICE TEST - 2

Question 41

Which service management practice is responsible for managing the process of identifying, documenting, and resolving the root cause of incidents and problems?

A) Incident Management

B) Problem Management

C) Change Management

D) Service Validation and Testing

Answer: B) Problem Management

Explanation: Problem Management is the service management practice responsible for managing the process of identifying, documenting, and resolving the root cause of incidents and problems. This practice focuses on identifying and addressing the underlying causes of incidents and problems to prevent future occurrences.

Question 42

Which service management practice is responsible for managing the process of planning, building, testing, and deploying new or changed IT services?

A) Service Design

B) Service Transition

C) Service Operation

D) Continual Service Improvement

Answer: B) Service Transition

Explanation: Service Transition is the service management practice responsible for managing the process of planning, building, testing, and deploying new or changed IT services. This practice focuses on ensuring that new or changed IT services are properly transitioned into production, minimizing disruption to existing services.

Question 43

Which service management practice is responsible for managing the process of capturing, documenting, and sharing knowledge and information across the organization?

A) Knowledge Management

B) Service Level Management

C) Service Desk

D) Continual Service Improvement

Answer: A) Knowledge Management

Explanation: Knowledge Management is the service management practice responsible for managing the process of capturing, documenting, and sharing knowledge and information across the organization. This practice focuses on ensuring that knowledge and information are properly captured, stored, and shared to support informed decision-making and improve IT services.

Question 44

Which service management practice is responsible for managing the process of identifying, prioritizing, and fulfilling user requests for new or changed IT services?

A) Service Request Management

B) Service Level Management

C) Change Management

D) Service Desk

Answer: A) Service Request Management

Explanation: Service Request Management is the service management practice responsible for managing the process of identifying, prioritizing, and fulfilling user requests for new or changed IT services. This practice focuses on ensuring that user requests are properly managed, prioritized, and fulfilled to meet business needs and expectations.

Question 45

What is the primary goal of the Incident Management process?

A) To restore normal service operation as quickly as possible

B) To identify and resolve the root cause of incidents

C) To manage and control IT service assets and configurations

D) To provide a single point of contact for user requests

Answer: A) To restore normal service operation as quickly as possible

Explanation: The primary goal of the Incident Management process is to restore normal service operation as quickly as possible, minimizing the impact on business operations and ensuring that IT services are available and accessible to users.

Question 46

Which of the following is a key activity in the Incident Management process?

A) Identifying and documenting the root cause of incidents

B) Assessing and managing the impact of incidents on business operations

C) Notifying and communicating with affected users and stakeholders

D) All of the above

Answer: D) All of the above

Explanation: All of the above activities are key components of the Incident Management process. Identifying and documenting the root cause of incidents helps to prevent future occurrences. Assessing and managing the impact of incidents on business operations ensures that the appropriate resources are allocated to resolve the incident. Notifying and communicating with affected users and stakeholders ensures that they are informed and updated throughout the incident resolution process.

Question 47

What is the purpose of the Incident Categorization process in Incident Management?

A) To assign a priority level to incidents based on their impact and urgency

B) To identify the root cause of incidents

C) To group incidents into categories for easier management and reporting

D) To escalate incidents to higher-level support teams

Answer: C) To group incidents into categories for easier management and reporting

Explanation: Incident Categorization is the process of grouping incidents into categories based on their type, severity, or other criteria. This helps to simplify incident management, enable more effective reporting and analysis, and improve incident resolution times.

Question 48

Which of the following is a key benefit of implementing a Major Incident Management process?

A) Faster resolution of minor incidents

B) Improved communication with users and stakeholders

C) Enhanced ability to manage high-impact, high-urgency incidents

D) Reduced need for incident reporting and analysis

Answer: C) Enhanced ability to manage high-impact, high-urgency incidents

Explanation: Major Incident Management is a specialized process for managing high-impact, high-urgency incidents that require immediate attention and resources. Implementing this process enables organizations to respond more effectively to critical incidents, minimizing their impact on business operations and reputation.

Question 49

What is the primary objective of the Change Control process?

A) To ensure that all changes are implemented as quickly as possible

B) To minimize the risk of disruptions to IT services

C) To ensure that all changes are properly assessed, approved, and implemented

D) To reduce the number of changes to IT services

Answer: C) To ensure that all changes are properly assessed, approved, and implemented

Explanation: The primary objective of the Change Control process is to ensure that all changes to IT services are properly assessed, approved, and implemented to minimize the risk of disruptions to IT services and ensure that changes align with business objectives.

Question 50

Which of the following is a key activity in the Change Control process?

A) Conducting post-implementation reviews to ensure that changes were successful

B) Identifying and documenting the root cause of incidents caused by changes

C) Assessing and evaluating the potential impact of changes on IT services

D) Developing and maintaining the change schedule

Answer: C) Assessing and evaluating the potential impact of changes on IT services

Explanation: Assessing and evaluating the potential impact of changes on IT services is a critical activity in the Change Control process. This involves analyzing the potential risks, benefits, and consequences of changes to ensure that they align with business objectives and do not disrupt IT services.

Question 51

What is the purpose of the Change Advisory Board (CAB) in the Change Control process?

A) To provide technical expertise for assessing and evaluating changes

B) To make final decisions on the approval or rejection of changes

C) To provide a forum for stakeholders to discuss and review changes

D) To ensure that changes are properly documented and recorded

Answer: C) To provide a forum for stakeholders to discuss and review changes

Explanation: The Change Advisory Board (CAB) is a group of stakeholders who review and discuss changes to ensure that they align with business objectives and do not disrupt IT services. The CAB provides a forum for stakeholders to share their expertise and concerns, ensuring that changes are properly assessed and evaluated.

Question 52

Which of the following is a key consideration when implementing an Emergency Change in the Change Control process?

A) Ensuring that the change is properly documented and recorded

B) Obtaining approval from the Change Advisory Board (CAB)

C) Assessing and evaluating the potential impact of the change on IT services

D) Minimizing the disruption to IT services and ensuring rapid implementation

Answer: D) Minimizing the disruption to IT services and ensuring rapid implementation

Explanation: Emergency Changes are implemented to resolve critical issues that require immediate attention. When implementing an Emergency Change, the key consideration is to minimize the disruption to IT services and ensure rapid implementation, while still ensuring that the change is properly assessed and evaluated to minimize risks.

Question 53

What is the primary goal of Architecture Management in IT service management?

A) To design and implement new IT services and solutions

B) To ensure that IT services align with business architecture and strategy

C) To manage and maintain existing IT infrastructure and applications

D) To optimize IT service delivery and support processes

Answer: B) To ensure that IT services align with business architecture and strategy

Explanation: Architecture Management is responsible for ensuring that IT services align with business architecture and strategy, enabling effective and efficient delivery of IT services that meet business needs.

Question 54

Which of the following is a key benefit of implementing Architecture Management in an organization?

A) Improved IT service delivery and support processes

B) Increased efficiency and effectiveness of IT operations

C) Better alignment of IT services with business strategy and objectives

D) Reduced costs and improved resource utilization

Answer: C) Better alignment of IT services with business strategy and objectives

Explanation: Architecture Management ensures that IT services are designed and delivered in alignment with business strategy and objectives, enabling organizations to achieve their goals and objectives more effectively. This results in better alignment of IT services with business needs, improved decision-making, and more effective use of IT resources.

Question 55

A large financial services company is planning to launch a new mobile banking app. The company's IT department is responsible for designing and delivering the underlying IT services to support the app. What should the IT department do to ensure that the IT services align with the business requirements for the mobile banking app?

A) Develop a comprehensive IT service catalog that includes the new mobile banking app

B) Conduct a thorough risk assessment to identify potential security threats to the app

C) Design an IT service architecture that aligns with the business architecture and strategy

D) Implement a robust IT service continuity plan to ensure minimal downtime

Answer: C) Design an IT service architecture that aligns with the business architecture and strategy

Explanation: To ensure that the IT services align with the business requirements for the mobile banking app, the IT department should design an IT service architecture that aligns with the business architecture and strategy. This involves understanding the business requirements and designing IT services that meet those requirements, ensuring that the IT services are fit for purpose and meet the needs of the business.

Question 56

A retail company is experiencing rapid growth and needs to scale its IT services to support increased demand. The company's IT department is responsible for ensuring that the IT services can scale to meet the increased demand. What should the IT department do to ensure that the IT services can scale effectively?

A) Implement a robust IT service monitoring and reporting system to track performance

B) Develop a comprehensive IT service catalog that includes scalable IT services

C) Design an IT service architecture that is flexible and scalable

D) Conduct a thorough risk assessment to identify potential scalability issues

Answer: C) Design an IT service architecture that is flexible and scalable

Explanation: To ensure that the IT services can scale effectively, the IT department should design an IT service architecture that is flexible and scalable. This involves designing IT services that can be easily scaled up or down to meet changing business demands, ensuring that the IT services are flexible and adaptable to changing business needs.

Question 57

A telecommunications company has implemented a new IT service management process for incident management. After three months, the company wants to evaluate the effectiveness of the new process.

What should the company do to determine whether the new process has improved incident resolution times?

A) Conduct a survey of IT staff to gather feedback on the new process

B) Analyze incident resolution times before and after the implementation of the new process

C) Compare the new process to industry best practices and standards

D) Identify and document lessons learned from the implementation of the new process

Answer: B) Analyze incident resolution times before and after the implementation of the new process

Explanation: To determine whether the new process has improved incident resolution times, the company should analyze incident resolution times before and after the implementation of the new process. This involves comparing metrics such as mean time to resolve (MTTR) or first contact resolution (FCR) rates to determine whether the new process has had a positive impact on incident resolution times.

Question 58

A healthcare organization wants to identify opportunities for improvement in its IT service management processes. What should the organization do to ensure that it identifies and prioritizes improvements that align with business objectives?

A) Conduct a thorough review of IT service management processes and identify areas for improvement

B) Engage with business stakeholders to understand their requirements and priorities

C) Analyze IT service management metrics and data to identify trends and areas for improvement

D) All of the above

Answer: D) All of the above

Explanation: To ensure that improvements align with business objectives, the organization should conduct a thorough review of IT service management processes, engage with business stakeholders, and analyze IT service management metrics and data. This involves taking a holistic approach to identify opportunities for improvement that align with business objectives and priorities.

Question 59

A financial services company has implemented a new IT service management tool to manage incident and problem management processes. After six months, the company wants to evaluate the effectiveness of the tool and identify opportunities for improvement. What should the company do to ensure that it gets the most out of the tool and identifies areas for improvement?

A) Conduct regular training sessions for IT staff on the use of the tool

B) Establish a governance structure to oversee the use of the tool

C) Define and track key performance indicators (KPIs) to measure the effectiveness of the tool

D) Engage with the tool vendor to identify best practices and new features

Answer: C) Define and track key performance indicators (KPIs) to measure the effectiveness of the tool

Explanation: To ensure that the company gets the most out of the tool and identifies areas for improvement, it should define and track KPIs to measure the effectiveness of the tool. This involves establishing metrics such as incident resolution rates, problem resolution rates, and user satisfaction to determine whether the tool is meeting its intended objectives.

Question 60

A retail company wants to improve its IT service continuity management process to ensure that IT services can be restored quickly in the event of a disaster. What should the company do to identify and prioritize improvements to the process?

A) Conduct a business impact analysis (BIA) to identify critical IT services

B) Develop a comprehensive IT service continuity plan that includes recovery strategies

C) Identify and assess risks to IT services and prioritize mitigation efforts

D) Engage with stakeholders to understand their requirements and priorities

Answer: A) Conduct a business impact analysis (BIA) to identify critical IT services

Explanation: To identify and prioritize improvements to the IT service continuity management process, the company should conduct a BIA to identify critical IT services that require rapid restoration in the event of a disaster. This involves understanding the business requirements and priorities to ensure that IT services are aligned with business needs.

Question 61

A telecommunications company wants to implement a chargeback model for its IT services, where business units are charged for the IT services they consume. What should the company do to ensure that the chargeback model is fair and transparent?

A) Establish a clear pricing strategy that reflects the cost of delivering IT services

B) Develop a comprehensive service catalog that includes detailed descriptions of IT services

C) Implement a robust service level management process to ensure that IT services meet business requirements

D) Engage with business stakeholders to understand their requirements and expectations

Answer: A) Establish a clear pricing strategy that reflects the cost of delivering IT services

Explanation: To ensure that the chargeback model is fair and transparent, the company should establish a clear pricing strategy that reflects the cost of delivering IT services. This involves understanding the costs associated with delivering IT services and developing a pricing model that is fair, transparent, and aligned with business objectives.

Question 62

A healthcare organization wants to optimize its IT budget to ensure that it is allocating resources effectively to support business objectives. What should the organization do to ensure that it is getting the best value from its IT budget?

A) Conduct a thorough analysis of IT costs and identify areas for cost optimization

B) Develop a comprehensive IT service portfolio that includes all IT services and their associated costs

C) Establish a robust service level management process to ensure that IT services meet business requirements

D) Engage with business stakeholders to understand their requirements and priorities

Answer: A) Conduct a thorough analysis of IT costs and identify areas for cost optimization

Explanation: To ensure that the organization is getting the best value from its IT budget, it should conduct a thorough analysis of IT costs and identify areas for cost optimization. This involves understanding where IT costs are being incurred and identifying opportunities to reduce costs without compromising IT service quality.

Question 63

A manufacturing company wants to implement a cost allocation model to charge business units for the IT services they consume. Which of the following cost allocation methods would be most suitable for this purpose?

A) Direct Cost Allocation: allocating costs directly to business units based on their usage

B) Indirect Cost Allocation: allocating costs to business units based on a predetermined percentage

C) Activity-Based Costing: allocating costs to business units based on the activities they perform

D) Zero-Based Budgeting: allocating costs to business units based on a zero-based budgeting approach

Answer: A) Direct Cost Allocation: allocating costs directly to business units based on their usage

Explanation: Direct Cost Allocation is the most suitable method for this purpose, as it allows for accurate allocation of costs to business units based on their actual usage of IT services.

Question 64

A financial services company wants to optimize its IT budget to ensure that it is investing in IT services that deliver the greatest business value. Which of the following financial management techniques would be most suitable for this purpose?

A) Cost-Benefit Analysis: evaluating the costs and benefits of IT services to determine their business value

B) Return on Investment (ROI) Analysis: evaluating the return on investment of IT services to determine their business value

C) Total Cost of Ownership (TCO) Analysis: evaluating the total cost of ownership of IT services to determine their business value

D) Break-Even Analysis: evaluating the break-even point of IT services to determine their business value

Answer: A) Cost-Benefit Analysis: evaluating the costs and benefits of IT services to determine their business value

Explanation: Cost-Benefit Analysis is the most suitable technique for this purpose, as it allows for a comprehensive evaluation of the costs and benefits of IT services to determine their business value and prioritize investments accordingly.

Question 65

A retail company has outsourced its IT service desk to a third-party supplier. What should the company do to ensure that the supplier is meeting its contractual obligations and delivering high-quality IT services?

A) Conduct regular service level management reviews with the supplier

B) Implement a robust supplier management process to monitor and control the supplier's performance

C) Develop a comprehensive contract that includes clear service level agreements (SLAs) and key performance indicators (KPIs)

D) Engage with the supplier's management team to build a strong relationship and ensure alignment with business objectives

Answer: B) Implement a robust supplier management process to monitor and control the supplier's performance

Explanation: Implementing a robust supplier management process is essential to ensure that the supplier is meeting its contractual obligations and delivering high-quality IT services. This involves monitoring and controlling the supplier's performance, managing risks, and ensuring that the supplier is aligned with business objectives.

Question 66

A healthcare organization is considering outsourcing its IT infrastructure management to a cloud services provider. What should the organization do to ensure that the cloud services provider is capable of meeting its IT service requirements?

A) Conduct a thorough due diligence assessment of the cloud services provider's capabilities and experience

B) Develop a comprehensive request for proposal (RFP) that includes clear IT service requirements and evaluation criteria

C) Engage with the cloud services provider's technical team to understand their architecture and service delivery model

D) Negotiate a robust contract that includes clear service level agreements (SLAs) and exit clauses

Answer: A) Conduct a thorough due diligence assessment of the cloud services provider's capabilities and experience

Explanation: Conducting a thorough due diligence assessment is essential to ensure that the cloud services provider is capable of meeting the organization's IT service requirements. This involves evaluating the provider's capabilities, experience, and reputation to ensure that they can deliver high-quality IT services that meet business needs.

Question 67

A technology company is experiencing a high turnover rate among its IT service management team members. What should the company do to improve employee retention and develop a stable workforce?

A) Offer competitive salaries and benefits to attract and retain top talent

B) Develop a comprehensive training and development program to enhance skills and knowledge

C) Implement a robust performance management process to identify and address performance issues

D) Foster a positive work culture and environment that supports employee engagement and well-being

Answer: D) Foster a positive work culture and environment that supports employee engagement and well-being

Explanation: Fostering a positive work culture and environment is crucial to improve employee retention and develop a stable workforce. This involves creating an environment that supports employee engagement, well-being, and job satisfaction, which can lead to increased loyalty and commitment to the organization.

Question 68

A financial services company is planning to implement a new IT service management tool that requires specialized skills and knowledge. What should the company do to ensure that its IT staff has the necessary skills and expertise to effectively use the new tool?

A) Recruit new staff members with the required skills and expertise

B) Develop a comprehensive training program to upskill existing staff members

C) Partner with the tool vendor to provide training and support

D) Outsource the implementation and management of the new tool to a third-party supplier

Answer: B) Develop a comprehensive training program to upskill existing staff members

Explanation: Developing a comprehensive training program is the most effective way to ensure that existing staff members have the necessary skills and expertise to effectively use the new tool. This involves identifying skill gaps, creating a training plan, and delivering training that meets the needs of the staff and the organization.

Question 69

A retail company has a contract with a supplier to provide IT services, but the supplier is consistently failing to meet the agreed-upon service levels. What should the company do to address this issue?

A) Renegotiate the contract to include more stringent service level agreements (SLAs)

B) Implement a robust monitoring and reporting process to track the supplier's performance

C) Engage with the supplier's management team to understand the root cause of the issue

D) Terminate the contract and find a new supplier

Answer: C) Engage with the supplier's management team to understand the root cause of the issue

Explanation: Engaging with the supplier's management team is the most effective way to address the issue, as it allows for a collaborative approach to understanding the root cause of the problem and identifying solutions. This approach also helps to maintain a positive relationship with the supplier.

Question 70

A healthcare organization is considering partnering with a new supplier to provide cloud services. What should the organization do to ensure that the supplier can meet its IT security and compliance requirements?

A) Conduct a thorough risk assessment and due diligence on the supplier

B) Review the supplier's security and compliance certifications and accreditations

C) Engage with the supplier's security and compliance team to understand their approach

D) Include specific security and compliance requirements in the contract

Answer: A) Conduct a thorough risk assessment and due diligence on the supplier

Explanation: Conducting a thorough risk assessment and due diligence is essential to ensure that the supplier can meet the organization's IT security and compliance requirements. This involves evaluating the supplier's security controls, compliance framework, and risk management practices to ensure they align with the organization's requirements.

Question 71

A software development company is planning to release a new version of its product, which includes significant changes to the user interface and functionality. What should the company do to ensure a smooth transition for its customers?

A) Develop a comprehensive release plan that includes testing, deployment, and communication strategies

B) Conduct thorough testing of the new version to identify and fix defects

C) Provide training and support to customers to help them adapt to the changes

D) Delay the release until all customers have been consulted and their feedback incorporated

Answer: A) Develop a comprehensive release plan that includes testing, deployment, and communication strategies

Explanation: Developing a comprehensive release plan is essential to ensure a smooth transition for customers. This plan should include testing, deployment, and communication strategies to manage the release effectively and minimize disruption to customers.

Question 72

A telecommunications company is releasing a new IT service that requires significant changes to its infrastructure and configuration. What should the company do to ensure that the release is properly documented and traceable?

A) Use a robust configuration management system to track changes to the infrastructure and configuration

B) Develop a comprehensive release document that includes details of the changes and testing results

C) Conduct a thorough impact assessment to identify and mitigate potential risks

D) Engage with stakeholders to ensure that they are informed and involved in the release process

Answer: A) Use a robust configuration management system to track changes to the infrastructure and configuration

Explanation: Using a robust configuration management system is essential to ensure that the release is properly documented and traceable. This system should track changes to the infrastructure and configuration, allowing for effective management and control of the release.

Question 73

A financial services company is planning to release a new mobile banking app that requires integration with its existing IT services. What should the company do to ensure that the release is properly coordinated and managed?

A) Establish a release management team to oversee the release process

B) Develop a comprehensive release plan that includes timelines, milestones, and dependencies

C) Conduct thorough testing of the app to ensure compatibility with existing IT services

D) Engage with stakeholders to ensure that they are informed and involved in the release process

Answer: B) Develop a comprehensive release plan that includes timelines, milestones, and dependencies

Explanation: Developing a comprehensive release plan is essential to ensure that the release is properly coordinated and managed. This plan should include timelines, milestones, and dependencies to ensure that all aspects of the release are properly managed and controlled.

Question 74

A healthcare organization is releasing a new electronic health record (EHR) system that requires significant changes to its IT infrastructure and clinical workflows. What should the organization do to ensure that the release is properly validated and verified?

A) Conduct thorough testing of the EHR system to ensure it meets functional and non-functional requirements

B) Engage with clinical stakeholders to validate the EHR system's clinical functionality and workflows

C) Develop a comprehensive validation and verification plan that includes testing, validation, and verification activities

D) Obtain regulatory approval for the EHR system before releasing it to production

Answer: C) Develop a comprehensive validation and verification plan that includes testing, validation, and verification activities

Explanation: Developing a comprehensive validation and verification plan is essential to ensure that the release is properly validated and verified. This plan should include testing, validation, and verification activities to ensure that the EHR system meets all requirements and is properly configured for production use.

Question 75

A technology company is releasing a new software update that requires deployment to multiple environments, including development, testing, and production. What should the company do to ensure that the release is properly controlled and deployed?

A) Use automated deployment tools to deploy the software update to all environments

B) Develop a comprehensive deployment plan that includes environment-specific configurations

C) Conduct thorough testing of the software update in each environment before deployment

D) Use a single, standardized environment for all deployments to simplify the process

Answer: B) Develop a comprehensive deployment plan that includes environment-specific configurations

Explanation: Developing a comprehensive deployment plan is essential to ensure that the release is properly controlled and deployed. This plan should include environment-specific configurations to ensure that the software update is properly deployed and configured for each environment.

Question 76

A retail company is releasing a new e-commerce platform that requires integration with its existing IT services, including payment processing and inventory management. What should the company do to ensure that the release is properly managed and coordinated?

A) Establish a release management team to oversee the release process

B) Develop a comprehensive release plan that includes timelines, milestones, and dependencies

C) Conduct thorough testing of the e-commerce platform to ensure compatibility with existing IT services

D) Use a phased release approach to deploy the e-commerce platform in stages

Answer: D) Use a phased release approach to deploy the e-commerce platform in stages

Explanation: Using a phased release approach is essential to ensure that the release is properly managed and coordinated. This approach allows for the deployment of the e-commerce platform in stages, reducing the risk of errors and ensuring that each stage is properly tested and validated before moving on to the next stage.

Question 77

A software development company is experiencing frequent defects and errors in its releases, resulting in delays and rework. What should the company do to improve its software quality and reduce defects?

A) Implement a robust testing and quality assurance process

B) Adopt an Agile development methodology to improve collaboration and flexibility

C) Use automated development tools to streamline coding and testing

D) Establish a DevOps culture to improve collaboration between development and operations teams

Answer: A) Implement a robust testing and quality assurance process

Explanation: Implementing a robust testing and quality assurance process is essential to improve software quality and reduce defects. This involves developing and executing comprehensive test cases, conducting regular code reviews, and ensuring that quality assurance activities are integrated throughout the development lifecycle.

Question 78

A financial services company is developing a new mobile banking app and wants to ensure that it is secure and compliant with regulatory requirements. What should the company do to ensure the app's security and compliance?

A) Conduct regular security testing and vulnerability assessments

B) Implement a secure coding practice and code review process

C) Engage with regulatory experts to ensure compliance with relevant regulations

D) Use a third-party security audit and compliance service

Answer: B) Implement a secure coding practice and code review process

Explanation: Implementing a secure coding practice and code review process is essential to ensure the app's security and compliance. This involves developing secure coding guidelines, conducting regular code reviews, and ensuring that developers are trained on secure coding practices to prevent vulnerabilities and ensure compliance.

Question 79

A healthcare organization is developing a new electronic health record (EHR) system and wants to ensure that it meets the needs of its clinicians and patients. What should the organization do to ensure that the EHR system is designed and developed with the needs of its users in mind?

A) Conduct user research and gather requirements from clinicians and patients

B) Develop a comprehensive technical specification for the EHR system

C) Engage with external experts to ensure compliance with regulatory requirements

D) Use an Agile development methodology to rapidly develop and deploy the EHR system

Answer: A) Conduct user research and gather requirements from clinicians and patients

Explanation: Conducting user research and gathering requirements from clinicians and patients is essential to ensure that the EHR system is designed and developed with the needs of its users in mind. This involves understanding the workflows, pain points, and requirements of clinicians and patients to develop an EHR system that meets their needs and improves patient care.

Question 80

A technology company is experiencing delays and cost overruns in its software development projects. What should the company do to improve its software development efficiency and effectiveness?

A) Implement a robust project management methodology to track progress and identify delays

B) Adopt a DevOps culture to improve collaboration between development and operations teams

C) Use automated development tools to streamline coding and testing

D) Establish a software development governance framework to ensure alignment with business objectives

Answer: D) Establish a software development governance framework to ensure alignment with business objectives

Explanation: Establishing a software development governance framework is essential to improve software development efficiency and effectiveness. This involves defining clear policies, procedures, and standards for software development, ensuring alignment with business objectives, and providing guidance and oversight to software development teams.

PRACTICE TEST - 3

A retail company is experiencing frequent downtime and performance issues with its e-commerce platform, resulting in lost sales and revenue. What should the company do to improve the availability and performance of its e-commerce platform?

A) Implement a robust monitoring and logging solution to identify and resolve issues quickly

B) Conduct a thorough capacity planning and management exercise to ensure sufficient resources

C) Develop a comprehensive disaster recovery plan to ensure business continuity

D) Engage with a third-party managed services provider to manage the e-commerce platform

Answer: B) Conduct a thorough capacity planning and management exercise to ensure sufficient resources

Explanation: Conducting a thorough capacity planning and management exercise is essential to improve the availability and performance of the e-commerce platform. This involves analyzing current and future resource requirements, identifying bottlenecks, and ensuring that sufficient resources are available to meet demand.

QUESTION 82

A financial services company is planning to migrate its core banking system to a cloud-based infrastructure. What should the company do to ensure a smooth and successful migration?

A) Conduct a thorough risk assessment and mitigation exercise to identify and address potential risks

B) Develop a comprehensive migration plan and timeline, including testing and validation

C) Engage with the cloud provider to ensure compliance with regulatory requirements

D) Establish a robust communication plan to inform stakeholders of the migration

Answer: B) Develop a comprehensive migration plan and timeline, including testing and validation

Explanation: Developing a comprehensive migration plan and timeline is essential to ensure a smooth and successful migration. This involves creating a detailed plan, including testing and validation, to ensure that the migration is executed correctly and with minimal disruption to business operations.

Question 83

A telecommunications company wants to measure the effectiveness of its incident management process. What should the company use as a key performance indicator (KPI) to measure the success of incident management?

A) Mean time to detect (MTTD)

B) Mean time to resolve (MTTR)

C) First contact resolution (FCR)

D) Customer satisfaction (CSAT)

Answer: B) Mean time to resolve (MTTR)

Explanation: Mean time to resolve (MTTR) is a key performance indicator (KPI) that measures the average time taken to resolve incidents. It is a critical metric to measure the effectiveness of incident management, as it directly impacts business operations and customer satisfaction.

Question 84

A healthcare organization wants to report on the value of its IT services to stakeholders. What should the organization use as a metric to demonstrate the value of IT services?

A) Return on investment (ROI)

B) Total cost of ownership (TCO)

C) Service level agreement (SLA) achievement

D) Customer satisfaction (CSAT)

Answer: A) Return on investment (ROI)

Explanation: Return on investment (ROI) is a metric that measures the financial return on investment in IT services. It demonstrates the value of IT services by showing the financial benefits achieved through the use of IT services, such as cost savings or revenue growth. This metric helps stakeholders understand the business value of IT services.

Question 85

A retail company wants to measure the effectiveness of its problem management process. What should the company use as a key performance indicator (KPI) to measure the success of problem management?

A) Number of problems resolved

B) Mean time to resolve (MTTR)

C) Problem resolution rate

D) Reduction in incidents caused by resolved problems

Answer: D) Reduction in incidents caused by resolved problems

Explanation: The reduction in incidents caused by resolved problems is a key performance indicator (KPI) that measures the effectiveness of problem management. It shows the impact of problem management on reducing the number of incidents, which is a critical metric to measure the success of problem management.

Question 86

A financial services company wants to report on the performance of its IT services to stakeholders. What should the company use as a reporting framework to provide a comprehensive view of IT service performance?

A) Balanced Scorecard (BSC)

B) ITIL 4 Service Value System (SVS)

C) COBIT 5

D) ISO/IEC 20000

Answer: B) ITIL 4 Service Value System (SVS)

Explanation: The ITIL 4 Service Value System (SVS) is a reporting framework that provides a comprehensive view of IT service performance. It includes six components: Engage, Design and Obtain/ Build, Obtain/Build, Deliver and Support, and Continual Improve and Align. The SVS framework helps organizations to report on the value of IT services and measure performance across the entire IT service lifecycle.

Question 87

A technology company is planning to implement a new cloud-based service. What should the company do to identify and manage risks associated with the implementation?

A) Conduct a thorough risk assessment and develop a risk register

B) Engage with the cloud provider to ensure compliance with regulatory requirements

C) Develop a comprehensive disaster recovery plan to ensure business continuity

D) Establish a robust monitoring and logging solution to detect security incidents

Answer: A) Conduct a thorough risk assessment and develop a risk register

Explanation: Conducting a thorough risk assessment and developing a risk register is essential to identify and manage risks associated with the implementation of a new cloud-based service. This involves identifying potential risks, assessing their likelihood and impact, and developing mitigation strategies to manage those risks.

Question 88

A healthcare organization is concerned about the risk of data breaches and cyber attacks on its IT systems. What should the organization do to manage this risk?

A) Implement a robust access control and identity management system

B) Develop a comprehensive incident response plan to respond to security incidents

C) Conduct regular security awareness training for employees

D) Engage with a third-party security expert to conduct a thorough security assessment

Answer: B) Develop a comprehensive incident response plan to respond to security incidents

Explanation: Developing a comprehensive incident response plan is essential to manage the risk of data breaches and cyber attacks. This involves developing a plan to quickly respond to security incidents, contain the damage, and restore normal operations. The plan should include procedures for incident detection, reporting, and response, as well as roles and responsibilities for incident response teams.

QUESTION 89

A financial services company is planning to merge with another company, which will result in the integration of their IT systems. What should the company do to manage the risks associated with this integration?

A) Conduct a thorough risk assessment and develop a risk register

B) Establish a robust testing and quality assurance process to ensure compatibility

C) Develop a comprehensive communication plan to inform stakeholders of the integration

D) Engage with a third-party expert to conduct a thorough technical assessment

Answer: A) Conduct a thorough risk assessment and develop a risk register

Explanation: Conducting a thorough risk assessment and developing a risk register is essential to manage the risks associated with the integration of IT systems. This involves identifying potential risks, assessing their likelihood and impact, and developing mitigation strategies to manage those risks.

Question 90

A retail company is concerned about the risk of supply chain disruptions impacting its IT services. What should the company do to manage this risk?

A) Develop a comprehensive business continuity plan to ensure continued operations

B) Establish a robust supplier management process to monitor supplier performance

C) Conduct regular risk assessments to identify and mitigate potential risks

D) Engage with a third-party expert to conduct a thorough supply chain risk assessment

Answer: B) Establish a robust supplier management process to monitor supplier performance

Explanation: Establishing a robust supplier management process is essential to manage the risk of supply chain disruptions. This involves monitoring supplier performance, assessing their risk profile, and developing mitigation strategies to manage potential risks. This helps to ensure that IT services are not impacted by supply chain disruptions.

Question 91

A telecommunications company is experiencing frequent incidents due to a lack of knowledge sharing among IT teams. What should the company do to improve knowledge management and reduce incidents?

A) Implement a comprehensive knowledge management system to store and share knowledge

B) Establish a robust training and development program to improve team skills

C) Conduct regular knowledge-sharing sessions and workshops

D) Engage with a third-party expert to conduct a thorough knowledge management assessment

Answer: A) Implement a comprehensive knowledge management system to store and share knowledge

Explanation: Implementing a comprehensive knowledge management system is essential to improve knowledge management and reduce incidents. This involves

---

CREATING A CENTRALIZED repository of knowledge, establishing processes for knowledge sharing, and ensuring that knowledge is easily accessible to IT teams.

Question 92

A healthcare organization is struggling to maintain accurate and up-to-date documentation of its IT services. What should the organization do to improve knowledge management and ensure accurate documentation?

A) Establish a robust documentation management process to ensure accuracy and currency

B) Implement a comprehensive knowledge management system to store and share knowledge

C) Conduct regular documentation audits to ensure compliance

D) Engage with a third-party expert to conduct a thorough documentation assessment

Answer: A) Establish a robust documentation management process to ensure accuracy and currency

Explanation: Establishing a robust documentation management process is essential to improve knowledge management and ensure accurate documentation. This involves creating processes for documenting IT services, ensuring that documentation is reviewed and updated regularly, and establishing controls to ensure accuracy and currency.

Question 93

A financial services company is experiencing difficulties in identifying and capturing knowledge from retiring employees. What should the company do to improve knowledge transfer and retention?

A) Implement a comprehensive knowledge transfer process to capture knowledge from retiring employees

B) Establish a robust mentoring program to pair retiring employees with newer staff

C) Conduct regular knowledge-sharing sessions and workshops

D) Engage with a third-party expert to conduct a thorough knowledge transfer assessment

Answer: A) Implement a comprehensive knowledge transfer process to capture knowledge from retiring employees

Explanation: Implementing a comprehensive knowledge transfer process is essential to improve knowledge transfer and retention. This involves creating a structured process to capture knowledge from retiring employees, including documentation, interviews, and training sessions.

Question 94

A technology company is struggling to maintain accurate and up-to-date information about its IT services in its service catalog. What should the company do to improve knowledge management and ensure accurate service information?

A) Establish a robust service catalog management process to ensure accuracy and currency

B) Implement a comprehensive knowledge management system to store and share knowledge

C) Conduct regular service catalog reviews to ensure compliance

D) Engage with a third-party expert to conduct a thorough service catalog assessment

Answer: A) Establish a robust service catalog management process to ensure accuracy and currency

Explanation: Establishing a robust service catalog management process is essential to improve knowledge management and ensure accurate service information. This involves creating processes for maintaining the service catalog, ensuring that information is reviewed and updated regularly, and establishing controls to ensure accuracy and currency.

Question 95

A retail company is experiencing frequent downtime and performance issues with its e-commerce platform due to inadequate resource allocation. What should the company do to improve resource utilization and ensure optimal performance?

A) Implement a robust capacity management process to ensure sufficient resources

B) Establish a comprehensive monitoring and logging solution to identify performance issues

C) Conduct regular resource utilization reviews to optimize resource allocation

D) Engage with a third-party expert to conduct a thorough resource utilization assessment

Answer: A) Implement a robust capacity management process to ensure sufficient resources

Explanation: Implementing a robust capacity management process is essential to improve resource utilization and ensure optimal performance. This involves analyzing current and future resource requirements, identifying bottlenecks, and ensuring that sufficient resources are allocated to meet demand.

Question 96

A healthcare organization is planning to migrate its core applications to a cloud-based infrastructure. What should the organization do to ensure a smooth and successful migration?

A) Conduct a thorough cloud readiness assessment to identify potential risks and opportunities

B) Establish a robust cloud governance framework to ensure compliance and control

C) Implement a comprehensive cloud migration plan to ensure minimal disruption

D) Engage with a third-party expert to conduct a thorough cloud migration assessment

Answer: C) Implement a comprehensive cloud migration plan to ensure minimal disruption

Explanation: Implementing a comprehensive cloud migration plan is essential to ensure a smooth and successful migration. This involves creating a detailed plan, including timelines, milestones, and risk mitigation strategies, to ensure minimal disruption to business operations.

Question 97

A telecommunications company is experiencing frequent network outages due to inadequate patch management. What should the company do to improve patch management and reduce network outages?

A) Implement a robust patch management process to ensure timely and effective patching

B) Establish a comprehensive vulnerability management program to identify and prioritize patches

C) Conduct regular network audits to identify and address patching gaps

D) Engage with a third-party expert to conduct a thorough patch management assessment

Answer: A) Implement a robust patch management process to ensure timely and effective patching

Explanation: Implementing a robust patch management process is essential to improve patch management and reduce network outages. This involves creating a structured process for patching, including testing, deployment, and verification, to ensure that patches are applied in a timely and effective manner.

Question 98

A financial services company is planning to implement a new database management system to improve data analytics capabilities. What should the company do to ensure a smooth and successful implementation?

A) Conduct a thorough database requirements analysis to identify and document requirements

B) Establish a robust database design and implementation process to ensure data integrity

C) Implement a comprehensive database testing and quality assurance process to ensure functionality

D) Engage with a third-party expert to conduct a thorough database implementation assessment

Answer: B) Establish a robust database design and implementation process to ensure data integrity

Explanation: Establishing a robust database design and implementation process is essential to ensure a smooth and successful implementation. This involves creating a structured process for designing and implementing the database, including data modeling, normalization, and data migration, to ensure that the database is properly designed and implemented to meet business requirements.

QUESTION 99

A retail company is planning to deploy a new point-of-sale (POS) system to all its stores. What should the company do to ensure a successful deployment?

A) Develop a comprehensive deployment plan, including timelines, milestones, and resource allocation

B) Conduct thorough testing and quality assurance to ensure the POS system meets requirements

C) Establish a robust training program to ensure store staff are proficient in using the new POS system

D) Engage with a third-party expert to conduct a thorough deployment assessment

Answer: A) Develop a comprehensive deployment plan, including timelines, milestones, and resource allocation

Explanation: Developing a comprehensive deployment plan is essential to ensure a successful deployment. This involves creating a detailed plan, including timelines, milestones, and resource allocation, to ensure that the deployment is executed smoothly and efficiently.

Question 100

A healthcare organization is deploying a new electronic health record (EHR) system to all its clinics. What should the organization do to minimize disruption to clinical services during the deployment?

A) Implement a phased deployment approach, deploying the EHR system to one clinic at a time

B) Conduct thorough testing and quality assurance to ensure the EHR system meets requirements

C) Establish a robust training program to ensure clinical staff are proficient in using the new EHR system

D) Engage with a third-party expert to conduct a thorough deployment assessment

Answer: A) Implement a phased deployment approach, deploying the EHR system to one clinic at a time

Explanation: Implementing a phased deployment approach is essential to minimize disruption to clinical services during the deployment. This involves deploying the EHR system to one clinic at a time, allowing for testing, validation, and training before moving on to the next clinic, to ensure that clinical services are not disrupted.

Question 101

A technology company is deploying a new software release to its customers. What should the company do to ensure that the deployment is properly documented and traceable?

A) Implement a robust deployment documentation process, including release notes and deployment plans

B) Establish a comprehensive change management process to ensure changes are properly assessed and approved

C) Conduct thorough testing and quality assurance to ensure the software release meets requirements

D) Engage with a third-party expert to conduct a thorough deployment assessment

Answer: A) Implement a robust deployment documentation process, including release notes and deployment plans

Explanation: Implementing a robust deployment documentation process is essential to ensure that the deployment is properly documented and traceable. This involves creating and maintaining accurate records of the deployment, including release notes, deployment plans, and configuration items, to ensure that the deployment can be tracked and audited.

Question 102

A financial services company is deploying a new IT service to its customers. What should the company do to ensure that the deployment meets the agreed-upon service level agreements (SLAs)?

A) Establish a comprehensive service validation process to ensure the IT service meets SLAs

B) Implement a robust monitoring and reporting process to ensure IT service performance is tracked

C) Conduct thorough testing and quality assurance to ensure the IT service meets requirements

D) Engage with a third-party expert to conduct a thorough deployment assessment

Answer: A) Establish a comprehensive service validation process to ensure the IT service meets SLAs

Explanation: Establishing a comprehensive service validation process is essential to ensure that the deployment meets the agreed-upon SLAs. This involves validating that the IT service meets the agreed-upon SLAs, including performance, availability, and functionality, to ensure that the IT service meets customer expectations.

Question 103

A retail company is deploying a new mobile application to its customers. What should the company do to ensure that the deployment is properly managed and controlled?

A) Establish a robust deployment management process, including planning, build, test, and deploy phases

B) Implement a comprehensive change management process to ensure changes are properly assessed and approved

C) Conduct thorough testing and quality assurance to ensure the mobile application meets requirements

D) Engage with a third-party expert to conduct a thorough deployment assessment

Answer: A) Establish a robust deployment management process, including planning, build, test, and deploy phases

Explanation: Establishing a robust deployment management process is essential to ensure that the deployment is properly managed and controlled. This involves creating a structured process, including planning, build, test, and deploy phases, to ensure that the deployment is executed smoothly and efficiently.

Question 104

A healthcare organization is deploying a new medical device to its clinics. What should the organization do to ensure that the deployment is properly verified and validated?

A) Implement a comprehensive verification and validation process to ensure the medical device meets requirements

B) Establish a robust testing and quality assurance process to ensure the medical device meets requirements

C) Conduct thorough training and documentation to ensure clinical staff are proficient in using the medical device

D) Engage with a third-party expert to conduct a thorough deployment assessment

Answer: A) Implement a comprehensive verification and validation process to ensure the medical device meets requirements

Explanation: Implementing a comprehensive verification and validation process is essential to ensure that the deployment is properly verified and validated. This involves verifying and validating that the medical device meets the agreed-upon requirements, including functionality, performance, and safety, to ensure that the medical device is properly deployed and meets clinical needs.

Question 105

A financial services company is deploying a new IT service to its customers. What should the company do to ensure that the deployment is properly coordinated and communicated?

A) Establish a robust deployment coordination process, including stakeholder management and communication plans

B) Implement a comprehensive change management process to ensure changes are properly assessed and approved

C) Conduct thorough testing and quality assurance to ensure the IT service meets requirements

D) Engage with a third-party expert to conduct a thorough deployment assessment

Answer: A) Establish a robust deployment coordination process, including stakeholder management and communication plans

Explanation: Establishing a robust deployment coordination process is essential to ensure that the deployment is properly coordinated and communicated. This involves creating a structured process, including stakeholder management and communication plans, to ensure that all stakeholders are informed and engaged throughout the deployment process.

Question 106

A technology company is deploying a new software release to its customers. What should the company do to ensure that the deployment is properly backed out in case of an issue?

A) Establish a robust back-out plan, including procedures for reversing changes and restoring previous versions

B) Implement a comprehensive testing and quality assurance process to ensure the software release meets requirements

C) Conduct thorough risk assessment and mitigation to identify and address potential issues

D) Engage with a third-party expert to conduct a thorough deployment assessment

Answer: A) Establish a robust back-out plan, including procedures for reversing changes and restoring previous versions

Explanation: Establishing a robust back-out plan is essential to ensure that the deployment can be properly backed out in case of an issue. This involves creating a structured plan, including procedures for reversing changes and restoring previous versions, to ensure that the deployment can be quickly and easily backed out if needed.

Question 107

A retail company is experiencing issues with its external service provider, leading to delays and disruptions in its IT services. What should the company do to improve the relationship and ensure better service delivery?

A) Establish a robust service level agreement (SLA) to define expectations and responsibilities

B) Implement a comprehensive communication plan to ensure regular updates and issue escalation

C) Conduct regular performance reviews and assessments to identify areas for improvement

D) Engage with a third-party expert to conduct a thorough relationship assessment

Answer: A) Establish a robust service level agreement (SLA) to define expectations and responsibilities

Explanation: Establishing a robust SLA is essential to improve the relationship and ensure better service delivery. This involves defining clear expectations and responsibilities, including service levels, performance metrics, and issue resolution processes, to ensure that both parties are aligned and working towards the same goals.

Question 108

A healthcare organization is looking to improve its relationships with its internal stakeholders, including clinical staff and business leaders. What should the organization do to build trust and ensure effective communication?

A) Establish a robust stakeholder management process to identify, analyze, and engage stakeholders

B) Implement a comprehensive communication plan to ensure regular updates and issue escalation

C) Conduct regular feedback sessions and surveys to understand stakeholder needs and concerns

D) Engage with a third-party expert to conduct a thorough relationship assessment

Answer: A) Establish a robust stakeholder management process to identify, analyze, and engage stakeholders

Explanation: Establishing a robust stakeholder management process is essential to build trust and ensure effective communication. This involves identifying, analyzing, and engaging stakeholders, including understanding their needs, concerns, and expectations, to ensure that their needs are met and their expectations are managed.

Question 109

A financial services company is experiencing issues with its IT services due to inaccurate configuration data. What should the company do to improve the accuracy and reliability of its configuration data?

A) Implement a robust configuration management system (CMS) to store and manage configuration data

B) Establish a comprehensive data validation and verification process to ensure accuracy

C) Conduct regular configuration audits to identify and correct errors

D) Engage with a third-party expert to conduct a thorough configuration assessment

Answer: A) Implement a robust configuration management system (CMS) to store and manage configuration data

Explanation: Implementing a robust CMS is essential to improve the accuracy and reliability of configuration data. This involves creating a centralized repository of configuration data, including details of IT assets, services, and relationships, to ensure that accurate and up-to-date information is available to support IT service management processes.

Question 110

A technology company is looking to improve its IT service continuity and disaster recovery capabilities. What should the company do to ensure that its configuration data is properly managed and maintained?

A) Establish a comprehensive configuration backup and recovery process to ensure data availability

B) Implement a robust configuration management system (CMS) to store and manage configuration data

C) Conduct regular configuration reviews and updates to ensure data accuracy and relevance

D) Engage with a third-party expert to conduct a thorough configuration assessment

Answer: A) Establish a comprehensive configuration backup and recovery process to ensure data availability

Explanation: Establishing a comprehensive configuration backup and recovery process is essential to ensure that configuration data is properly managed and maintained. This involves creating regular backups of configuration data, testing recovery processes, and ensuring that data can be quickly restored in the event of a disaster or major outage.

Question 109

A financial services company is experiencing issues with its IT services due to inaccurate configuration data. What should the company do to improve the accuracy and reliability of its configuration data?

A) Implement a robust configuration management system (CMS) to store and manage configuration data

B) Establish a comprehensive configuration management process to ensure data accuracy and consistency

C) Conduct regular configuration audits and reviews to identify and correct errors

D) Engage with a third-party expert to conduct a thorough configuration assessment

Answer: B) Establish a comprehensive configuration management process to ensure data accuracy and consistency

Explanation: Establishing a comprehensive configuration management process is essential to improve the accuracy and reliability of configuration data. This involves creating a structured process, including data collection, validation, and updating, to ensure that configuration data is accurate, consistent, and up-to-date.

Question 110

A technology company is planning to implement a new IT service, which requires the configuration of multiple infrastructure components. What should the company do to ensure that the configuration is properly documented and managed?

A) Create a comprehensive configuration model to document the configuration of infrastructure components

B) Implement a robust change management process to ensure changes are properly assessed and approved

C) Conduct thorough testing and quality assurance to ensure the configuration meets requirements

D) Engage with a third-party expert to conduct a thorough configuration assessment

Answer: A) Create a comprehensive configuration model to document the configuration of infrastructure components

Explanation: Creating a comprehensive configuration model is essential to ensure that the configuration is properly documented and managed. This involves creating a detailed model, including configuration items, relationships, and dependencies, to ensure that the configuration is accurately documented and can be easily managed and updated.

Question 111

A retail company is designing a new e-commerce platform to support its online sales channel. What should the company do to ensure that the platform is designed to meet the needs of its customers?

A) Conduct thorough market research and analysis to understand customer needs and preferences

B) Establish a comprehensive service catalog to define and document IT services

C) Implement a robust service level management process to ensure agreed-upon service levels

D) Engage with a third-party expert to conduct a thorough service design assessment

Answer: A) Conduct thorough market research and analysis to understand customer needs and preferences

Explanation: Conducting thorough market research and analysis is essential to ensure that the platform is designed to meet the needs of its customers. This involves gathering and analyzing data on customer needs, preferences, and behaviors to inform the design of the platform and ensure that it meets customer expectations.

Question 112

A healthcare organization is designing a new telemedicine service to support remote patient care. What should the organization do to ensure that the service is designed to meet the required levels of availability and reliability?

A) Establish a comprehensive availability and capacity management process to ensure sufficient resources

B) Implement a robust IT service continuity management process to ensure business continuity

C) Conduct thorough testing and quality assurance to ensure the service meets requirements

D) Engage with a third-party expert to conduct a thorough service design assessment

Answer: A) Establish a comprehensive availability and capacity management process to ensure sufficient resources

Explanation: Establishing a comprehensive availability and capacity management process is essential to ensure that the service is designed to meet the required levels of availability and reliability. This involves analyzing current and future resource requirements, identifying potential bottlenecks, and ensuring that sufficient resources are allocated to meet demand.

Question 113

A financial services company is designing a new mobile banking application to support its customers. What should the company do to ensure that the application is designed to meet the required levels of security and compliance?

A) Establish a comprehensive information security management process to ensure secure design

B) Implement a robust service validation and testing process to ensure requirements are met

C) Conduct thorough risk assessment and mitigation to identify and address potential security risks

D) Engage with a third-party expert to conduct a thorough security assessment

Answer: A) Establish a comprehensive information security management process to ensure secure design

Explanation: Establishing a comprehensive information security management process is essential to ensure that the application is designed to meet the required levels of security and compliance. This involves implementing security controls, conducting security risk assessments, and ensuring that the design meets relevant security standards and regulations.

Question 114

A technology company is designing a new cloud-based service to support its customers. What should the company do to ensure that the service is designed to meet the required levels of scalability and performance?

A) Establish a comprehensive capacity and performance management process to ensure sufficient resources

B) Implement a robust service design process to ensure scalable and performant design

C) Conduct thorough testing and quality assurance to ensure the service meets requirements

D) Engage with a third-party expert to conduct a thorough performance assessment

Answer: B) Implement a robust service design process to ensure scalable and performant design

Explanation: Implementing a robust service design process is essential to ensure that the service is designed to meet the required levels of scalability and performance. This involves designing the service to be scalable, flexible, and performant, and ensuring that the design meets relevant architectural and technical standards.

Question 113

A financial services company is designing a new mobile banking application to support its customers' financial transactions. What should the company do to ensure that the application is designed to meet the required levels of security and compliance?

A) Establish a comprehensive information security management process to ensure data protection

B) Implement a robust IT service continuity management process to ensure business continuity

C) Conduct thorough testing and quality assurance to ensure the application meets requirements

D) Engage with a third-party expert to conduct a thorough service design assessment

Answer: A) Establish a comprehensive information security management process to ensure data protection

Explanation: Establishing a comprehensive information security management process is essential to ensure that the application is designed to meet the required levels of security and compliance. This involves identifying and mitigating potential security risks, implementing controls to protect data, and ensuring compliance with relevant regulations and standards.

Question 114

A technology company is designing a new cloud-based IT service to support its customers' business operations. What should the company do to ensure that the service is designed to meet the required levels of scalability and flexibility?

A) Establish a comprehensive capacity management process to ensure sufficient resources

B) Implement a robust service level management process to ensure agreed-upon service levels

C) Conduct thorough testing and quality assurance to ensure the service meets requirements

D) Engage with a third-party expert to conduct a thorough service design assessment

Answer: A) Establish a comprehensive capacity management process to ensure sufficient resources

Explanation: Establishing a comprehensive capacity management process is essential to ensure that the service is designed to meet the required levels of scalability and flexibility. This involves analyzing current and future resource requirements, identifying potential bottlenecks, and ensuring that sufficient resources are allocated to meet demand and support business growth.

Question 115

A retail company is planning to release a new version of its e-commerce platform, which includes significant changes to its user interface and functionality. What should the company do to ensure a smooth transition to the new release?

A) Develop a comprehensive release plan, including timelines, milestones, and resource allocation

B) Implement a robust testing and quality assurance process to ensure the release meets requirements

C) Establish a comprehensive communication plan to inform stakeholders of the release

D) Engage with a third-party expert to conduct a thorough release assessment

Answer: A) Develop a comprehensive release plan, including timelines, milestones, and resource allocation

Explanation: Developing a comprehensive release plan is essential to ensure a smooth transition to the new release. This involves creating a detailed plan, including timelines, milestones, and resource allocation, to ensure that the release is properly managed and executed.

Question 116

A healthcare organization is releasing a new version of its electronic health record (EHR) system, which includes significant changes to its clinical functionality. What should the organization do to ensure that the release is properly validated and verified?

A) Implement a robust testing and quality assurance process to ensure the release meets requirements

B) Establish a comprehensive validation and verification process to ensure clinical safety and effectiveness

C) Develop a comprehensive release plan, including timelines, milestones, and resource allocation

D) Engage with a third-party expert to conduct a thorough release assessment

Answer: B) Establish a comprehensive validation and verification process to ensure clinical safety and effectiveness

Explanation: Establishing a comprehensive validation and verification process is essential to ensure that the release is properly validated and verified. This involves creating a structured process, including clinical validation and verification, to ensure that the release meets clinical requirements and is safe and effective for use.

Question 117

A technology company is planning to release a new version of its software product, which includes significant changes to its architecture and functionality. What should the company do to ensure that the release is properly documented and traceable?

A) Establish a comprehensive documentation management process to ensure accurate and up-to-date documentation

B) Implement a robust testing and quality assurance process to ensure the release meets requirements

C) Develop a comprehensive release plan, including timelines, milestones, and resource allocation

D) Engage with a third-party expert to conduct a thorough release assessment

Answer: A) Establish a comprehensive documentation management process to ensure accurate and up-to-date documentation

Explanation: Establishing a comprehensive documentation management process is essential to ensure that the release is properly documented and traceable. This involves creating a structured process, including documentation templates, version control, and approval processes, to ensure that accurate and up-to-date documentation is available for the release.

Question 118

A financial services company is releasing a new version of its online banking platform, which includes significant changes to its security and compliance features. What should the company do to ensure that the release is properly assessed and approved?

A) Implement a robust risk assessment and mitigation process to identify and address potential risks

B) Establish a comprehensive change management process to ensure changes are properly assessed and approved

C) Develop a comprehensive release plan, including timelines, milestones, and resource allocation

D) Engage with a third-party expert to conduct a thorough release assessment

Answer: B) Establish a comprehensive change management process to ensure changes are properly assessed and approved

Explanation: Establishing a comprehensive change management process is essential to ensure that the release is properly assessed and approved. This involves creating a structured process, including change request submission, impact assessment, and approval processes, to ensure that changes are properly evaluated and authorized before release.

Question 119

A retail company is experiencing recurring incidents related to its e-commerce platform, resulting in significant downtime and lost sales. What should the company do to improve its knowledge management and reduce the likelihood of future incidents?

A) Establish a comprehensive knowledge management process to capture and share knowledge

B) Implement a robust incident management process to quickly resolve incidents

C) Develop a comprehensive training program to improve staff skills and knowledge

D) Engage with a third-party expert to conduct a thorough knowledge assessment

Answer: A) Establish a comprehensive knowledge management process to capture and share knowledge

Explanation: Establishing a comprehensive knowledge management process is essential to improve knowledge management and reduce the likelihood of future incidents. This involves creating a structured process, including knowledge capture, documentation, and sharing, to ensure that knowledge is accurately captured, stored, and made available to support incident resolution and problem management.

Question 120

A healthcare organization is implementing a new electronic health record (EHR) system, which requires significant changes to its clinical processes and procedures. What should the organization do to ensure that its staff has access to accurate and up-to-date knowledge and information?

A) Develop a comprehensive training program to improve staff skills and knowledge

B) Establish a comprehensive knowledge management process to capture and share knowledge

C) Implement a robust communication plan to inform staff of changes and updates

D) Engage with a third-party expert to conduct a thorough knowledge assessment

Answer: B) Establish a comprehensive knowledge management process to capture and share knowledge

Explanation: Establishing a comprehensive knowledge management process is essential to ensure that staff has access to accurate and up-to-date knowledge and information. This involves creating a structured process, including knowledge capture, documentation, and sharing, to ensure that knowledge is accurately captured, stored, and made available to support staff training and adoption of the new EHR system.

PRACTICE TEST - 4

Question 121

A financial services company is experiencing issues with its IT services due to inadequate resource allocation and capacity planning. What should the company do to ensure that its IT resources are properly allocated and utilized?

A) Implement a robust capacity management process to ensure sufficient resources

B) Establish a comprehensive resource allocation process to ensure effective utilization

C) Develop a comprehensive service level agreement (SLA) to define service expectations

D) Engage with a third-party expert to conduct a thorough resource assessment

Answer: B) Establish a comprehensive resource allocation process to ensure effective utilization

Explanation: Establishing a comprehensive resource allocation process is essential to ensure that IT resources are properly allocated and utilized. This involves creating a structured process, including resource request management, allocation, and tracking, to ensure that resources are effectively utilized and aligned with business needs.

Question 122

A technology company is experiencing issues with its IT services due to inadequate monitoring and event management. What should the company do to ensure that its IT services are properly monitored and managed?

A) Implement a robust monitoring and event management process to detect and respond to events

B) Establish a comprehensive incident management process to quickly resolve incidents

C) Develop a comprehensive service level agreement (SLA) to define service expectations

D) Engage with a third-party expert to conduct a thorough service assessment

Answer: A) Implement a robust monitoring and event management process to detect and respond to events

Explanation: Implementing a robust monitoring and event management process is essential to ensure that IT services are properly monitored and managed. This involves creating a structured process, including event detection, notification, and response, to ensure that events are quickly detected and responded to, minimizing the impact on IT services.

Question 123

A retail company's IT department is experiencing a high volume of incidents related to its e-commerce platform, resulting in significant downtime and lost sales. However, the incidents are intermittent and difficult to reproduce, making it challenging to identify the root cause. What should the company do to address this issue?

A) Implement a robust incident management process to quickly resolve incidents

B) Establish a comprehensive problem management process to identify and address root causes

C) Develop a comprehensive testing and quality assurance process to identify defects

D) Engage with a third-party expert to conduct a thorough incident analysis

Answer: B) Establish a comprehensive problem management process to identify and address root causes

Explanation: Establishing a comprehensive problem management process is essential to address intermittent and difficult-to-reproduce incidents. This involves creating a structured process, including problem identification, analysis, and resolution, to ensure that root causes are identified and addressed, reducing the likelihood of future incidents.

Question 124

A healthcare organization's IT department is experiencing a high volume of service requests related to its electronic health record (EHR) system, resulting in significant delays and user frustration. However, the service requests are often unclear or incomplete, leading to misunderstandings and miscommunication. What should the organization do to address this issue?

A) Implement a robust service request management process to quickly fulfill requests

B) Establish a comprehensive service catalog to define and communicate services

C) Develop a comprehensive communication plan to clarify service requests

D) Engage with a third-party expert to conduct a thorough service request analysis

Answer: B) Establish a comprehensive service catalog to define and communicate services

Explanation: Establishing a comprehensive service catalog is essential to address unclear or incomplete service requests. This involves creating a structured catalog, including service descriptions, requirements, and expectations, to ensure that users understand what services are available and how to request them, reducing misunderstandings and miscommunication.

Question 125

A financial services company's IT department is experiencing a high volume of changes related to its trading platform, resulting in significant risk and instability. However, the changes are often urgent and must be implemented quickly to respond to changing market conditions. What should the company do to balance the need for speed with the need for stability?

A) Implement a robust change management process to ensure thorough assessment and approval

B) Establish a comprehensive emergency change process to expedite urgent changes

C) Develop a comprehensive risk management process to identify and mitigate risks

D) Engage with a third-party expert to conduct a thorough change management assessment

Answer: B) Establish a comprehensive emergency change process to expedite urgent changes

Explanation: Establishing a comprehensive emergency change process is essential to balance the need for speed with the need for stability. This involves creating a structured process, including expedited assessment, approval, and implementation, to ensure that urgent changes are implemented quickly while minimizing risk and instability.

Question 126

A technology company's IT department is experiencing a high volume of incidents related to its cloud-based services, resulting in significant downtime and user frustration. However, the incidents are often caused by complex interactions between multiple cloud services and third-party providers. What should the company do to address this issue?

A) Implement a robust incident management process to quickly resolve incidents

B) Establish a comprehensive problem management process to identify and address root causes

C) Develop a comprehensive service dependency mapping process to understand complex interactions

D) Engage with a third-party expert to conduct a thorough incident analysis

Answer: C) Develop a comprehensive service dependency mapping process to understand complex interactions

Explanation: Developing a comprehensive service dependency mapping process is essential to address incidents caused by complex interactions between multiple cloud services and third-party providers. This involves creating a detailed map, including dependencies and relationships, to ensure that IT staff understand how services interact and can quickly identify and address root causes.

Question 127

A retail company's IT department is experiencing a high volume of service requests related to its e-commerce platform, resulting in significant delays and user frustration. However, the service requests are often related to customizations and configurations that are not properly documented or tracked. What should the company do to address this issue?

A) Implement a robust service request management process to quickly fulfill requests

B) Establish a comprehensive configuration management process to track and manage configurations

C) Develop a comprehensive knowledge management process to document and share knowledge

D) Engage with a third-party expert to conduct a thorough service request analysis

Answer: B) Establish a comprehensive configuration management process to track and manage configurations

Explanation: Establishing a comprehensive configuration management process is essential to address service requests related to customizations and configurations. This involves creating a structured process, including configuration tracking, management, and documentation, to ensure that IT staff understand the current state of configurations and can quickly fulfill service requests.

Question 128

A healthcare organization's IT department is experiencing a high volume of incidents related to its electronic health record (EHR)

system, resulting in significant downtime and patient safety risks. However, the incidents are often caused by complex interactions between multiple systems and stakeholders, including clinical staff, IT staff, and third-party vendors. What should the organization do to address this issue?

A) Implement a robust incident management process to quickly resolve incidents

B) Establish a comprehensive problem management process to identify and address root causes

C) Develop a comprehensive communication plan to improve collaboration and communication

D) Engage with a third-party expert to conduct a thorough incident analysis

Answer: C) Develop a comprehensive communication plan to improve collaboration and communication

Explanation: Developing a comprehensive communication plan is essential to address incidents caused by complex interactions between multiple systems and stakeholders. This involves creating a structured plan, including communication protocols, roles, and responsibilities, to ensure that all stakeholders are informed and aligned, and can quickly respond to incidents.

Question 129

A financial services company's IT department is experiencing a high volume of changes related to its trading platform, resulting in significant risk and instability. However, the changes are often driven by regulatory requirements, which can be unclear or open to interpretation. What should the company do to ensure that changes are properly assessed and implemented?

A) Implement a robust change management process to ensure thorough assessment and approval

B) Establish a comprehensive compliance management process to ensure regulatory adherence

C) Develop a comprehensive risk management process to identify and mitigate risks

D) Engage with a third-party expert to conduct a thorough regulatory analysis

Answer: B) Establish a comprehensive compliance management process to ensure regulatory adherence

Explanation: Establishing a comprehensive compliance management process is essential to ensure that changes are properly assessed and implemented in response to regulatory requirements. This involves creating a structured process, including regulatory tracking, interpretation, and implementation, to ensure that IT staff understand regulatory requirements and can implement changes that meet those requirements.

Question 130

A technology company's IT department is experiencing a high volume of incidents related to its cloud-based services, resulting in significant downtime and user frustration. However, the incidents are often caused by issues with third-party cloud providers, which can be difficult to resolve due to contractual and technical complexities. What should the company do to address this issue?

A) Implement a robust incident management process to quickly resolve incidents

B) Establish a comprehensive supplier management process to manage third-party providers

C) Develop a comprehensive service level management process to define and manage service levels

D) Engage with a third-party expert to conduct a thorough incident analysis

Answer: B) Establish a comprehensive supplier management process to manage third-party providers

Explanation: Establishing a comprehensive supplier management process is essential to address incidents caused by issues with third-party cloud providers. This involves creating a structured process, including supplier selection, contracting, and management, to ensure that IT staff can effectively manage third-party providers and resolve incidents quickly.

Question 131

A retail company's IT department is experiencing a high volume of service requests related to its e-commerce platform, resulting in significant delays and user frustration. However, the service requests are often related to new or changing business requirements, which can be unclear or evolving. What should the company do to ensure that service requests are properly understood and fulfilled?

A) Implement a robust service request management process to quickly fulfill requests

B) Establish a comprehensive business relationship management process to understand business requirements

C) Develop a comprehensive service level management process to define and manage service levels

D) Engage with a third-party expert to conduct a thorough business analysis

Answer: B) Establish a comprehensive business relationship management process to understand business requirements

Explanation: Establishing a comprehensive business relationship management process is essential to ensure that service requests are properly understood and fulfilled in response to new or changing business requirements. This involves creating a structured process, including business relationship management, requirement gathering, and service design, to ensure that IT staff understand business needs and can design and deliver services that meet those needs.

Question 132

A healthcare organization's IT department is experiencing a high volume of incidents related to its electronic health record (EHR) system, resulting in significant downtime and patient safety risks. However, the incidents are often caused by complex interactions between multiple systems and stakeholders, including clinical staff, IT staff, and third-party vendors. What should the organization do to address this issue?

A) Implement a robust incident management process to quickly resolve incidents

B) Establish a comprehensive problem management process to identify and address root causes

C) Develop a comprehensive communication plan to improve collaboration and communication

D) Engage with a third-party expert to conduct a thorough incident analysis

Answer: C) Develop a comprehensive communication plan to improve collaboration and communication

Explanation: Developing a comprehensive communication plan is essential to address incidents caused by complex interactions between multiple systems and stakeholders. This involves creating a structured plan, including communication protocols, roles, and responsibilities, to ensure that all stakeholders are informed and aligned, and can quickly respond to incidents.

Question 133

A financial services company's IT department is experiencing a high volume of changes related to its trading platform, resulting in significant risk and instability. However, the changes are often driven by competing business priorities, which can lead to conflicting requirements and stakeholder expectations. What should the company do to ensure that changes are properly prioritized and managed?

A) Implement a robust change management process to ensure thorough assessment and approval

B) Establish a comprehensive stakeholder management process to manage expectations and requirements

C) Develop a comprehensive prioritization framework to prioritize changes based on business value

D) Engage with a third-party expert to conduct a thorough business analysis

Answer: C) Develop a comprehensive prioritization framework to prioritize changes based on business value

Explanation: Developing a comprehensive prioritization framework is essential to ensure that changes are properly prioritized and managed in response to competing business priorities. This involves creating a structured framework, including criteria and weights, to prioritize changes based on business value, risk, and other factors, ensuring that changes are aligned with business objectives.

Question 134

A technology company's IT department is experiencing a high volume of incidents related to its cloud-based services, resulting in significant downtime and user frustration. However, the incidents are often caused by issues with third-party cloud providers, which can be difficult to resolve due to technical complexities and vendor relationships. What should the company do to address this issue?

A) Implement a robust incident management process to quickly resolve incidents

B) Establish a comprehensive supplier management process to manage third-party providers

C) Develop a comprehensive technical debt management process to address underlying technical issues

D) Engage with a third-party expert to conduct a thorough technical analysis

Answer: C) Develop a comprehensive technical debt management process to address underlying technical issues

Explanation: Developing a comprehensive technical debt management process is essential to address incidents caused by issues with third-party cloud providers. This involves creating a structured process, including technical debt identification, prioritization, and remediation, to address underlying technical issues and improve the overall health and resilience of cloud-based services.

Question 135

A retail company's IT department is experiencing a high volume of service requests related to its e-commerce platform, resulting in significant delays and user frustration. However, the service requests are often related to new or changing business requirements, which can be unclear or evolving. What should the company do to ensure that service requests are properly understood and fulfilled?

A) Implement a robust service request management process to quickly fulfill requests

B) Establish a comprehensive business relationship management process to understand business requirements

C) Develop a comprehensive service catalog to define and communicate services

D) Engage with a third-party expert to conduct a thorough business analysis

Answer: B) Establish a comprehensive business relationship management process to understand business requirements

Explanation: Establishing a comprehensive business relationship management process is essential to ensure that service requests are properly understood and fulfilled in response to new or changing business requirements. This involves creating a structured process, including business relationship management, requirement gathering, and service design, to ensure that IT staff understand business needs and can design and deliver services that meet those needs.

Question 136

A healthcare organization's IT department is experiencing a high volume of incidents related to its electronic health record (EHR) system, resulting in significant downtime and patient safety risks. However, the incidents are often caused by complex interactions between multiple systems and stakeholders, including clinical staff, IT staff, and third-party vendors. What should the organization do to address this issue?

A) Implement a robust incident management process to quickly resolve incidents

B) Establish a comprehensive problem management process to identify and address root causes

C) Develop a comprehensive collaboration framework to improve communication and coordination

D) Engage with a third-party expert to conduct a thorough incident analysis

Answer: C) Develop a comprehensive collaboration framework to improve communication and coordination

Explanation: Developing a comprehensive collaboration framework is essential to address incidents caused by complex interactions between multiple systems and stakeholders. This involves creating a structured framework, including roles, responsibilities, and communication protocols, to ensure that all stakeholders are informed and aligned, and can quickly respond to incidents.

Question 137

An organization is adopting Agile and DevOps practices to improve the speed and quality of its software development and deployment processes. However, the IT service management team is struggling to adapt its traditional incident management process to the new Agile/DevOps environment. What should the organization do to address this challenge?

A) Implement a robust incident management process to quickly resolve incidents

B) Establish a comprehensive continuous integration and continuous delivery (CI/CD) pipeline

C) Develop a comprehensive collaboration framework to improve communication and coordination between development and operations teams

D) Engage with a third-party expert to conduct a thorough Agile/DevOps assessment

Answer: C) Develop a comprehensive collaboration framework to improve communication and coordination between development and operations teams

Explanation: Developing a comprehensive collaboration framework is essential to adapt incident management to the Agile/DevOps environment. This involves creating a structured framework, including roles, responsibilities, and communication protocols, to ensure that development and operations teams are aligned and can quickly respond to incidents.

Question 138

An organization is using Agile and DevOps practices to develop and deploy its software applications. However, the IT service management team is struggling to ensure that the new applications meet the required service levels and quality standards. What should the organization do to address this challenge?

A) Implement a robust service level management process to define and manage service levels

B) Establish a comprehensive continuous testing and continuous monitoring process

C) Develop a comprehensive service validation and testing process to ensure quality and service levels

D) Engage with a third-party expert to conduct a thorough Agile/ DevOps assessment

Answer: C) Develop a comprehensive service validation and testing process to ensure quality and service levels

Explanation: Developing a comprehensive service validation and testing process is essential to ensure that new applications meet the required service levels and quality standards in the Agile/DevOps environment. This involves creating a structured process, including testing, validation, and quality assurance, to ensure that applications meet business requirements and service levels.

Question 139

An organization is designing a new IT service to support its business operations. However, the service design team is struggling to ensure that the new service meets the required business outcomes and service levels. What should the organization do to address this challenge?

A) Implement a robust service design process to ensure business outcomes and service levels

B) Establish a comprehensive business relationship management process to understand business requirements

C) Develop a comprehensive service catalog to define and communicate services

D) Engage with a third-party expert to conduct a thorough business analysis

Answer: A) Implement a robust service design process to ensure business outcomes and service levels

Explanation: Implementing a robust service design process is essential to ensure that the new service meets the required business outcomes and service levels. This involves creating a structured process, including service design, validation, and testing, to ensure that the service meets business requirements and service levels.

Question 140

An organization is transitioning a new IT service into production. However, the transition team is struggling to ensure that the new service is properly tested, validated, and deployed. What should the organization do to address this challenge?

A) Implement a robust transition planning and support process to ensure smooth transition

B) Establish a comprehensive change management process to manage changes

C) Develop a comprehensive testing and validation process to ensure quality and service levels

D) Engage with a third-party expert to conduct a thorough transition assessment

Answer: A) Implement a robust transition planning and support process to ensure smooth transition

Explanation: Implementing a robust transition planning and support process is essential to ensure that the new service is properly tested, validated, and deployed. This involves creating a structured process, including transition planning, testing, validation, and deployment, to ensure that the service is transitioned smoothly into production.

Question 141

An organization is planning to obtain a new IT service from a third-party provider. However, the procurement team is struggling to ensure that the new service meets the required business outcomes and service levels. What should the organization do to address this challenge?

A) Develop a comprehensive service level agreement (SLA) to define and manage service levels

B) Establish a comprehensive supplier management process to manage third-party providers

C) Implement a robust procurement process to ensure business outcomes and service levels

D) Engage with a third-party expert to conduct a thorough procurement assessment

Answer: C) Implement a robust procurement process to ensure business outcomes and service levels

Explanation: Implementing a robust procurement process is essential to ensure that the new service meets the required business outcomes and service levels. This involves creating a structured process, including procurement planning, supplier selection, and contract management, to ensure that the service meets business requirements and service levels.

Question 142

An organization is building a new IT service in-house. However, the development team is struggling to ensure that the new service meets the required business outcomes and service levels. What should the organization do to address this challenge?

A) Develop a comprehensive service design package (SDP) to define and manage service levels

B) Establish a comprehensive project management process to manage service development

C) Implement a robust service build process to ensure business outcomes and service levels

D) Engage with a third-party expert to conduct a thorough service development assessment

Answer: C) Implement a robust service build process to ensure business outcomes and service levels

Explanation: Implementing a robust service build process is essential to ensure that the new service meets the required business outcomes and service levels. This involves creating a structured process, including service build, testing, validation, and deployment, to ensure that the service meets business requirements and service levels.

Question 143

An organization's IT service is experiencing a major incident that is impacting critical business operations. However, the incident management team is struggling to quickly resolve the incident due to a lack of effective communication and collaboration between teams. What should the organization do to address this challenge?

A) Implement a robust incident management process to quickly resolve incidents

B) Establish a comprehensive communication plan to improve communication and collaboration

C) Develop a comprehensive incident escalation process to ensure timely escalation

D) Engage with a third-party expert to conduct a thorough incident management assessment

Answer: B) Establish a comprehensive communication plan to improve communication and collaboration

Explanation: Establishing a comprehensive communication plan is essential to quickly resolve major incidents that impact critical business operations. This involves creating a structured plan, including communication protocols, roles, and responsibilities, to ensure that all stakeholders are informed and aligned, and can quickly respond to incidents.

Question 144

An organization's IT service is experiencing a high volume of incidents related to a specific application. However, the incident management team is struggling to identify the root cause of the incidents due to a lack of effective problem management processes. What should the organization do to address this challenge?

A) Implement a robust incident management process to quickly resolve incidents

B) Establish a comprehensive problem management process to identify and address root causes

C) Develop a comprehensive incident reporting process to improve incident reporting

D) Engage with a third-party expert to conduct a thorough incident analysis

Answer: B) Establish a comprehensive problem management process to identify and address root causes

Explanation: Establishing a comprehensive problem management process is essential to identify and address the root cause of incidents related to a specific application. This involves creating a structured process, including problem identification, analysis, and resolution, to ensure that the root cause is identified and addressed, reducing the likelihood of future incidents.

Question 145

An organization is implementing ITIL 4 to improve its IT service management capabilities. However, the organization is struggling to identify and design its value streams and processes. What should the organization do to address this challenge?

A) Conduct a thorough business analysis to identify business requirements and value streams

B) Establish a comprehensive process design framework to design and implement processes

C) Develop a comprehensive value stream mapping process to identify and design value streams

D) Engage with a third-party expert to conduct a thorough ITIL 4 implementation assessment

Answer: C) Develop a comprehensive value stream mapping process to identify and design value streams

Explanation: Developing a comprehensive value stream mapping process is essential to identify and design value streams and processes. This involves creating a structured process, including value stream identification, mapping, and design, to ensure that value streams and processes are aligned with business requirements and outcomes.

Question 146

An organization has designed and implemented its value streams and processes. However, the organization is struggling to ensure that its processes are operating effectively and efficiently. What should the organization do to address this challenge?

A) Establish a comprehensive process governance framework to ensure process adherence

B) Develop a comprehensive process performance measurement framework to measure process performance

C) Implement a comprehensive process optimization framework to optimize process performance

D) Engage with a third-party expert to conduct a thorough process assessment

Answer: B) Develop a comprehensive process performance measurement framework to measure process performance

Explanation: Developing a comprehensive process performance measurement framework is essential to ensure that processes are operating effectively and efficiently. This involves creating a structured framework, including process metrics, measurement, and reporting, to ensure that process performance is measured and optimized, aligning with business outcomes and requirements.

Question 147

An organization is outsourcing some of its IT services to a third-party supplier. However, the organization is struggling to ensure that the supplier is meeting the required service levels and quality standards. What should the organization do to address this challenge?

A) Establish a comprehensive supplier management process to manage supplier performance

B) Develop a comprehensive service level agreement (SLA) to define and manage service levels

C) Implement a comprehensive contract management process to manage contracts

D) Engage with a third-party expert to conduct a thorough supplier assessment

Answer: A) Establish a comprehensive supplier management process to manage supplier performance

Explanation: Establishing a comprehensive supplier management process is essential to ensure that the supplier is meeting the required service levels and quality standards. This involves creating a structured process, including supplier selection, contract management, and performance monitoring, to ensure that suppliers are managed effectively and efficiently.

Question 148

An organization is partnering with a third-party organization to deliver a new IT service. However, the organization is struggling to ensure that the partnership is aligned with business requirements and outcomes. What should the organization do to address this challenge?

A) Develop a comprehensive partnership agreement to define and manage partnership terms

B) Establish a comprehensive business relationship management process to manage business relationships

C) Implement a comprehensive partnership management process to manage partnership performance

D) Engage with a third-party expert to conduct a thorough partnership assessment

Answer: C) Implement a comprehensive partnership management process to manage partnership performance

Explanation: Implementing a comprehensive partnership management process is essential to ensure that the partnership is aligned with business requirements and outcomes. This involves creating a structured process, including partnership planning, performance monitoring, and issue resolution, to ensure that partnerships are managed effectively and efficiently.

Question 149

An organization is struggling to understand the needs and expectations of its service consumers. What should the organization do to address this challenge?

A) Conduct a thorough service consumer analysis to understand their needs and expectations

B) Establish a comprehensive service catalog to communicate services to consumers

C) Implement a comprehensive feedback and complaint management process to capture consumer feedback

D) Engage with a third-party expert to conduct a thorough consumer research study

Answer: A) Conduct a thorough service consumer analysis to understand their needs and expectations

Explanation: Conducting a thorough service consumer analysis is essential to understand the needs and expectations of service consumers. This involves gathering and analyzing data on consumer behavior, preferences, and pain points to ensure that services are designed and delivered to meet their needs.

Question 150

An organization has designed and delivered a new IT service, but is struggling to ensure that service consumers are adopting and using the service effectively. What should the organization do to address this challenge?

A) Develop a comprehensive user adoption plan to drive service adoption

B) Establish a comprehensive training and support program to enable consumer success

C) Implement a comprehensive communication plan to promote the service to consumers

D) Engage with a third-party expert to conduct a thorough service adoption assessment

Answer: B) Establish a comprehensive training and support program to enable consumer success

Explanation: Establishing a comprehensive training and support program is essential to ensure that service consumers are adopting and using the service effectively. This involves creating a structured program, including training, documentation, and support, to enable consumers to use the service successfully and achieve their desired outcomes.

Question 151

An organization is struggling to create value for its customers through its IT services. What should the organization do to address this challenge?

A) Focus on improving the efficiency and effectiveness of its IT processes

B) Engage with customers to understand their needs and co-create value

C) Invest in new technologies to improve the quality of its IT services

D) Reduce the cost of its IT services to increase customer satisfaction

Answer: B) Engage with customers to understand their needs and co-create value

Explanation: Engaging with customers to understand their needs and co-create value is essential to create value for customers through IT services. This involves working collaboratively with customers to understand their needs, preferences, and pain points, and designing and delivering services that meet those needs.

Question 152

An organization has designed and delivered an IT service that meets the needs of its customers, but is struggling to ensure that the service continues to create value over time. What should the organization do to address this challenge?

A) Continuously monitor and evaluate customer feedback to identify areas for improvement

B) Focus on maintaining the stability and reliability of the IT service

C) Invest in new technologies to improve the quality of the IT service

D) Reduce the cost of the IT service to increase customer satisfaction

Answer: A) Continuously monitor and evaluate customer feedback to identify areas for improvement

Explanation: Continuously monitoring and evaluating customer feedback is essential to ensure that the IT service continues to create value over time. This involves gathering and analyzing customer feedback, identifying areas for improvement, and making changes to the service to ensure it remains aligned with customer needs and preferences.

Question 153

An organization is developing a new product that will be supported by an IT service. What should the organization do to ensure that the product and service are aligned?

A) Develop the product and service separately, with minimal collaboration between teams

B) Engage in joint product and service development, with ongoing collaboration between teams

C) Focus on developing the product, and then develop the supporting service afterwards

D) Develop a comprehensive product roadmap, and then develop the supporting service

Answer: B) Engage in joint product and service development, with ongoing collaboration between teams

Explanation: Engaging in joint product and service development, with ongoing collaboration between teams, is essential to ensure that the product and service are aligned. This involves working collaboratively to design and develop the product and service, ensuring that they meet customer needs and are delivered effectively.

Question 154

An organization has a portfolio of IT services that are no longer meeting customer needs. What should the organization do to address this challenge?

A) Continuously maintain and update the existing services

B) Retire the existing services and develop new ones

C) Engage with customers to understand their changing needs and modify the services accordingly

D) Reduce the cost of the existing services to increase customer satisfaction

Answer: C) Engage with customers to understand their changing needs and modify the services accordingly

Explanation: Engaging with customers to understand their changing needs and modifying the services accordingly is essential to address the challenge of IT services no longer meeting customer needs. This involves gathering and analyzing customer feedback, identifying areas for improvement, and making changes to the services to ensure they remain aligned with customer needs and preferences.

Question 155

An organization is struggling to maintain an accurate and up-to-date service catalogue. What should the organization do to address this challenge?

A) Assign a single person to be responsible for maintaining the service catalogue

B) Implement a comprehensive service catalogue management process

C) Focus on maintaining technical documentation instead of a service catalogue

D) Use a static document to manage the service catalogue

Answer: B) Implement a comprehensive service catalogue management process

Explanation: Implementing a comprehensive service catalogue management process is essential to maintain an accurate and up-to-date service catalogue. This involves establishing a structured process for creating, updating, and maintaining the service catalogue, including roles, responsibilities, and governance.

Question 156

An organization has a service catalogue that is not being used effectively by customers. What should the organization do to address this challenge?

A) Improve the technical accuracy of the service catalogue

B) Enhance the user experience of the service catalogue

C) Increase the number of services listed in the service catalogue

D) Reduce the accessibility of the service catalogue

Answer: B) Enhance the user experience of the service catalogue

Explanation: Enhancing the user experience of the service catalogue is essential to ensure it is used effectively by customers. This involves designing and delivering a user-friendly service catalogue that meets customer needs, including clear service descriptions, easy navigation, and effective search functionality.

Question 157

An organization is struggling to meet its service level agreements (SLAs) due to inadequate resource allocation. What should the organization do to address this challenge?

A) Increase the resources allocated to IT services without assessing the impact

B) Conduct a thorough service level management process to identify and address resource gaps

C) Reduce the scope of services to reduce resource requirements

D) Ignore the SLAs and focus on other IT priorities

Answer: B) Conduct a thorough service level management process to identify and address resource gaps

Explanation: Conducting a thorough service level management process is essential to identify and address resource gaps that are impacting SLAs. This involves assessing current resource allocation, identifying gaps, and making adjustments to ensure that resources are aligned with service level requirements.

Question 158

An organization has implemented a service level management process, but is struggling to ensure that services are delivered consistently to meet customer expectations. What should the organization do to address this challenge?

A) Focus on improving the technical quality of IT services

B) Establish a comprehensive continuous improvement program to identify and address service inconsistencies

C) Increase the frequency of service level reporting to improve visibility

D) Reduce the number of service level agreements to simplify management

Answer: B) Establish a comprehensive continuous improvement program to identify and address service inconsistencies

Explanation: Establishing a comprehensive continuous improvement program is essential to identify and address service inconsistencies that impact customer expectations. This involves regularly reviewing service performance, identifying areas for improvement, and implementing changes to ensure consistent service delivery.

Question 159

An organization is designing a new IT service that must meet specific business requirements. What should the organization focus on to ensure the service provides utility to customers?

A) Ensuring the service is delivered at the lowest possible cost

B) Ensuring the service meets the specified functional requirements

C) Ensuring the service is delivered with the required capacity and performance

D) Ensuring the service is delivered with the required security and compliance

Answer: C) Ensuring the service is delivered with the required capacity and performance

Explanation: Ensuring the service is delivered with the required capacity and performance is essential to provide utility to customers. Utility refers to the ability of a service to meet customer needs and deliver the required outcomes. Capacity and performance are critical aspects of utility, as they directly impact the ability of the service to meet customer requirements.

Question 160

An organization is struggling to ensure that its IT services consistently meet the required levels of reliability, availability, and maintainability. What should the organization focus on to improve the warranty of its services?

A) Implementing a comprehensive testing program to ensure service quality

B) Establishing a robust incident management process to quickly resolve issues

C) Developing a comprehensive service continuity plan to ensure service availability

D) Implementing a comprehensive service design process to ensure service reliability and maintainability

Answer: D) Implementing a comprehensive service design process to ensure service reliability and maintainability

Explanation: Implementing a comprehensive service design process is essential to improve the warranty of IT services. Warranty refers to the ability of a service to meet customer expectations for reliability, availability, maintainability, and other aspects of service quality. A comprehensive service design process ensures that services are designed to meet the required levels of warranty, reducing the risk of service failures and issues.

PRACTICE TEST - 5

Question 161

An organization is implementing ITIL 4 to improve its IT service management capabilities. However, the organization's IT services are heavily reliant on third-party vendors. Which of the following approaches would be most effective in addressing this issue?

A) Implementing a vendor management system to monitor and control vendor performance

B) Conducting a vendor risk assessment to identify and mitigate potential risks

C) Establishing a collaborative vendor management approach, involving multiple stakeholders

D) Implementing a hybrid vendor management model, combining internal and external resources

Answer: D) Implementing a hybrid vendor management model, combining internal and external resources

Explanation: Implementing a hybrid vendor management model enables the organization to leverage internal and external resources, ensuring effective management of third-party vendors and IT services.

Question 162

An IT service provider is experiencing issues with its service level management process, resulting in poor customer satisfaction. However, the organization's customers have varying and conflicting service level expectations. Which of the following approaches would be most effective in addressing this issue?

A) Implementing a service level management framework that accounts for customer variability

B) Conducting a customer expectations analysis to understand and prioritize customer needs

C) Establishing a dynamic service level management approach, adapting to changing customer expectations

D) Implementing a machine learning-powered service level management tool to predict customer needs

Answer: C) Establishing a dynamic service level management approach, adapting to changing customer expectations

Explanation: Establishing a dynamic service level management approach enables the organization to adapt to changing customer expectations, ensuring that IT services meet customer needs and improve customer satisfaction.

Question 163

An organization is implementing ITIL 4 to improve its IT service management capabilities. However, the organization's IT services are experiencing frequent incidents due to complex technical dependencies. Which of the following approaches would be most effective in addressing this issue?

A) Implementing a technical debt management program to reduce technical complexity

B) Conducting a dependency mapping exercise to identify and mitigate technical dependencies

C) Establishing a DevOps culture to improve collaboration and communication between teams

D) Implementing an AI-powered incident management tool to automate incident resolution

Answer: B) Conducting a dependency mapping exercise to identify and mitigate technical dependencies

Explanation: Conducting a dependency mapping exercise helps identify and mitigate technical dependencies, reducing the likelihood of incidents and improving IT service stability.

Question 164

An IT service provider is experiencing issues with its continuous improvement process, resulting in limited improvements to IT services. However, the organization has limited resources and budget for improvement initiatives. Which of the following approaches would be most effective in addressing this issue?

A) Implementing a lean IT approach to eliminate waste and optimize resources

B) Conducting a cost-benefit analysis to prioritize improvement initiatives

C) Establishing a crowdsourcing platform to solicit improvement ideas from employees

D) Implementing a continuous improvement framework that leverages existing resources

Answer: D) Implementing a continuous improvement framework that leverages existing resources

Explanation: Implementing a continuous improvement framework that leverages existing resources enables the organization to improve IT services without requiring significant additional resources or budget.

Question 165

An organization is implementing ITIL 4 to improve its IT service management capabilities. However, the organization's IT services are experiencing frequent changes due to shifting business requirements. Which of the following approaches would be most effective in addressing this issue?

A) Implementing a change management process that includes business stakeholders

B) Conducting a business impact analysis to identify and prioritize changes

C) Establishing a culture of continuous change and experimentation

D) Implementing an Agile-based change management approach to adapt to changing requirements

Answer: D) Implementing an Agile-based change management approach to adapt to changing requirements

Explanation: Implementing an Agile-based change management approach enables the organization to adapt quickly to changing business requirements, ensuring that IT services remain aligned with business needs.

QUESTION 166

An IT service provider is experiencing issues with its service desk function, resulting in poor customer satisfaction. However, the organization's service desk team is already working at maximum capacity. Which of the following approaches would be most effective in addressing this issue?

A) Implementing a chatbot-powered service desk solution to automate customer interactions

B) Conducting a root cause analysis of service desk issues to identify and address underlying causes

C) Establishing a shift-left approach to empower end-users to resolve issues independently

D) Implementing a knowledge management system to improve service desk efficiency

Answer: C) Establishing a shift-left approach to empower end-users to resolve issues independently

Explanation: Establishing a shift-left approach empowers end-users to resolve issues independently, reducing the workload on the service desk team and improving customer satisfaction.

Question 167

What is the primary purpose of the ITIL 4 "Engage" practice?

A) To design and develop IT services that meet business requirements

B) To deliver and support IT services to meet agreed-upon service levels

C) To engage with stakeholders to understand their needs and expectations

D) To monitor and control IT services to ensure they meet agreed-upon service levels

Answer: C) To engage with stakeholders to understand their needs and expectations

Explanation: The ITIL 4 "Engage" practice focuses on engaging with stakeholders to understand their needs and expectations, ensuring that IT services meet business requirements and deliver value.

Question 168

Which of the following ITIL 4 practices is responsible for ensuring that IT services are delivered and supported in a way that meets agreed-upon service levels?

A) Design and Transition

B) Obtain/Build

C) Deliver and Support

D) Engage

Answer: C) Deliver and Support

Explanation: The ITIL 4 "Deliver and Support" practice ensures that IT services are delivered and supported to meet agreed-upon service levels, providing value to customers and stakeholders.

Question 169

Describe the purpose and scope of the ITIL 4 "Design and Transition" practice.

A) To design and develop IT services that meet business requirements, and transition them into production

B) To deliver and support IT services to meet agreed-upon service levels, and monitor their performance

C) To engage with stakeholders to understand their needs and expectations, and design IT services accordingly

D) To obtain and build IT services that meet business requirements, and deliver them to customers

Answer: A) To design and develop IT services that meet business requirements, and transition them into production

Explanation: The ITIL 4 "Design and Transition" practice focuses on designing and developing IT services that meet business requirements, and transitioning them into production, ensuring a seamless handover to the delivery and support teams.

Question 170

Describe the key activities and objectives of the ITIL 4 "Deliver and Support" practice.

A) To design and develop IT services, and transition them into production

B) To deliver and support IT services to meet agreed-upon service levels, and monitor their performance

C) To engage with stakeholders to understand their needs and expectations, and design IT services accordingly

D) To obtain and build IT services that meet business requirements, and deliver them to customers

Answer: B) To deliver and support IT services to meet agreed-upon service levels, and monitor their performance

Explanation: The ITIL 4 "Deliver and Support" practice focuses on delivering and supporting IT services to meet agreed-upon service levels, and monitoring their performance, ensuring that IT services deliver value to customers and stakeholders.

Question 171

An organization is implementing ITIL 4 to improve its IT service management capabilities. The organization has a complex IT infrastructure with multiple stakeholders, services, and vendors. How can the organization ensure effective service integration and management across its IT services?

A) Implement a service integration and management (SIAM) framework to coordinate IT services

B) Establish a single point of contact for all IT services to simplify communication

C) Conduct a thorough risk assessment to identify potential service integration issues

D) Develop a comprehensive IT service catalog to showcase IT services to stakeholders

Answer: A) Implement a service integration and management (SIAM) framework to coordinate IT services

Explanation: Implementing a SIAM framework enables the organization to coordinate IT services effectively, ensuring seamless integration and management across multiple stakeholders, services, and vendors.

Question 172

An IT service provider is experiencing issues with its service level management process, resulting in poor customer satisfaction. The organization has multiple IT services with varying service level agreements (SLAs). How can the organization improve its service level management process to meet customer expectations?

A) Implement a service level management framework that accounts for customer variability

B) Conduct a thorough analysis of customer expectations to understand their needs

C) Establish a continuous monitoring and reporting process to track service level performance

D) Develop a comprehensive service level agreement template for all IT services

Answer: A) Implement a service level management framework that accounts for customer variability

Explanation: Implementing a service level management framework that accounts for customer variability enables the organization to tailor its IT services to meet individual customer needs, improving customer satisfaction and loyalty.

Question 173

An organization is implementing ITIL 4 to improve its IT service management capabilities. The organization has a complex global IT infrastructure with multiple regions, languages, and cultures. How can the organization ensure effective IT service management across its global operations?

A) Implement a global IT service management framework that accounts for regional variations

B) Establish a centralized IT service management team to oversee global operations

C) Conduct a thorough analysis of regional IT service management maturity levels

D) Develop a comprehensive IT service management training program for global staff

Answer: A) Implement a global IT service management framework that accounts for regional variations

Explanation: Implementing a global IT service management framework that accounts for regional variations enables the organization to adapt its IT service management approach to meet local needs, ensuring effective IT service delivery across its global operations.

Question 174

An IT service provider is experiencing issues with its continuous improvement process, resulting in limited improvements to IT services. The organization has a large IT service portfolio with multiple stakeholders and vendors. How can the organization improve its continuous improvement process to drive meaningful IT service enhancements?

A) Implement a continuous improvement framework that engages stakeholders and vendors

B) Conduct a thorough analysis of IT service performance metrics to identify areas for improvement

C) Establish a culture of continuous improvement and experimentation within the organization

D) Develop a comprehensive IT service improvement roadmap with clear objectives and timelines

Answer: A) Implement a continuous improvement framework that engages stakeholders and vendors

Explanation: Implementing a continuous improvement framework that engages stakeholders and vendors enables the organization to leverage collective expertise and resources, driving meaningful IT service enhancements and improving overall IT service quality.

Question 175

An organization is implementing ITIL 4 to improve its IT service management capabilities. The organization has a complex IT infrastructure with multiple cloud services, vendors, and integrations.

How can the organization ensure effective IT service management in a multi-cloud environment?

A) Implement a cloud service management framework that integrates with existing ITSM processes

B) Establish a cloud center of excellence to oversee cloud service management

C) Conduct a thorough analysis of cloud service providers to ensure compliance with ITSM standards

D) Develop a comprehensive cloud service catalog to showcase cloud services to stakeholders

Answer: A) Implement a cloud service management framework that integrates with existing ITSM processes

Explanation: Implementing a cloud service management framework that integrates with existing ITSM processes enables the organization to manage cloud services effectively, ensuring seamless integration with existing IT services and processes.

Question 176

An IT service provider is experiencing issues with its service desk function, resulting in poor customer satisfaction. The organization has a large IT service portfolio with multiple stakeholders, vendors, and languages. How can the organization improve its service desk function to meet diverse customer needs?

A) Implement a service desk framework that supports multiple languages and channels

B) Establish a global service desk team to support customers across regions

C) Conduct a thorough analysis of customer feedback to identify service desk improvements

D) Develop a comprehensive service desk knowledge base to support customer inquiries

Answer: A) Implement a service desk framework that supports multiple languages and channels

Explanation: Implementing a service desk framework that supports multiple languages and channels enables the organization to provide effective support to customers with diverse needs, improving customer satisfaction and loyalty.

Question 177

An organization is implementing ITIL 4 to improve its IT service management capabilities. The organization has a complex digital transformation initiative with multiple stakeholders, services, and vendors. How can the organization ensure effective IT service management during digital transformation?

A) Implement a digital transformation framework that integrates with existing ITSM processes

B) Establish a digital transformation office to oversee IT service management

C) Conduct a thorough analysis of digital transformation impacts on IT services

D) Develop a comprehensive digital transformation roadmap with clear ITSM objectives

Answer: A) Implement a digital transformation framework that integrates with existing ITSM processes

Explanation: Implementing a digital transformation framework that integrates with existing ITSM processes enables the organization to manage IT services effectively during digital transformation, ensuring minimal disruption to business operations.

Question 178

An IT service provider is experiencing issues with its IT service continuity management process, resulting in poor business resilience. The organization has a large IT service portfolio with multiple stakeholders, vendors, and dependencies. How can the organization improve its IT service continuity management process to ensure business resilience?

A) Implement an IT service continuity management framework that accounts for business dependencies

B) Establish a business continuity management team to oversee IT service continuity

C) Conduct a thorough analysis of IT service continuity risks and impacts

D) Develop a comprehensive IT service continuity plan with clear recovery objectives

Answer: A) Implement an IT service continuity management framework that accounts for business dependencies

Explanation: Implementing an IT service continuity management framework that accounts for business dependencies enables the organization to ensure business resilience by managing IT service continuity effectively, minimizing the impact of disruptions on business operations.

Question 179

An organization is implementing ITIL 4 to improve its IT service management capabilities. The organization has a complex IT infrastructure with multiple artificial intelligence (AI) and machine learning (ML) applications. How can the organization ensure effective IT service management for AI and ML applications?

A) Implement an AI and ML service management framework that integrates with existing ITSM processes

B) Establish an AI and ML center of excellence to oversee IT service management

C) Conduct a thorough analysis of AI and ML application dependencies and impacts

D) Develop a comprehensive AI and ML service catalog to showcase services to stakeholders

Answer: A) Implement an AI and ML service management framework that integrates with existing ITSM processes

Explanation: Implementing an AI and ML service management framework that integrates with existing ITSM processes enables the organization to manage AI and ML applications effectively, ensuring seamless integration with existing IT services and processes.

Question 180

An IT service provider is experiencing issues with its IT asset management process, resulting in poor IT asset utilization and compliance. The organization has a large IT asset portfolio with multiple stakeholders, vendors, and dependencies. How can the organization improve its IT asset management process to ensure effective IT asset utilization and compliance?

A) Implement an IT asset management framework that accounts for asset lifecycles and dependencies

B) Establish an IT asset management team to oversee asset utilization and compliance

C) Conduct a thorough analysis of IT asset utilization and compliance risks and impacts

D) Develop a comprehensive IT asset management plan with clear objectives and timelines

Answer: A) Implement an IT asset management framework that accounts for asset lifecycles and dependencies

Explanation: Implementing an IT asset management framework that accounts for asset lifecycles and dependencies enables the organization to manage IT assets effectively, ensuring optimal utilization, compliance, and minimizing waste and costs.

Question 181

An organization is implementing ITIL 4 to improve its IT service management capabilities. The organization has a complex global IT infrastructure with multiple time zones, languages, and cultures. How can the organization ensure effective IT service management across its global operations?

A) Implement a global IT service management framework that accounts for regional variations

B) Establish a follow-the-sun service management approach to ensure 24/7 coverage

C) Conduct a thorough analysis of global IT service management maturity levels

D) Develop a comprehensive global IT service management training program

Answer: B) Establish a follow-the-sun service management approach to ensure 24/7 coverage

Explanation: Establishing a follow-the-sun service management approach enables the organization to provide seamless IT service management coverage across global operations, ensuring minimal disruption to business operations.

Question 182

An IT service provider is experiencing issues with its IT service catalog management process, resulting in poor customer satisfaction. The organization has a large IT service portfolio with multiple stakeholders, vendors, and dependencies. How can the organization improve its IT service catalog management process to ensure effective IT service delivery?

A) Implement an IT service catalog management framework that accounts for service dependencies

B) Establish a service catalog management team to oversee service delivery

C) Conduct a thorough analysis of IT service catalog requirements and stakeholder needs

D) Develop a comprehensive IT service catalog with clear service descriptions and pricing

Answer: C) Conduct a thorough analysis of IT service catalog requirements and stakeholder needs

Explanation: Conducting a thorough analysis of IT service catalog requirements and stakeholder needs enables the organization to develop an effective IT service catalog that meets customer needs, improving customer satisfaction and loyalty.

Question 183

An organization is implementing ITIL 4 to improve its IT service management capabilities. The organization has a complex IT infrastructure with multiple cloud services, vendors, and integrations.

How can the organization ensure effective IT service management in a multi-cloud environment?

A) Implement a cloud service management framework that integrates with existing ITSM processes

B) Establish a cloud governance model to oversee cloud service management

C) Conduct a thorough analysis of cloud service provider capabilities and risks

D) Develop a comprehensive cloud service management plan with clear objectives and timelines

Answer: B) Establish a cloud governance model to oversee cloud service management

Explanation: Establishing a cloud governance model enables the organization to oversee cloud service management effectively, ensuring compliance with organizational policies, standards, and regulatory requirements.

Question 184

An IT service provider is experiencing issues with its IT service continuity management process, resulting in poor business resilience. The organization has a large IT service portfolio with multiple stakeholders, vendors, and dependencies. How can the organization improve its IT service continuity management process to ensure business resilience?

A) Implement an IT service continuity management framework that accounts for business dependencies

B) Establish a business continuity management team to oversee IT service continuity

C) Conduct a thorough analysis of IT service continuity risks and impacts on business operations

D) Develop a comprehensive IT service continuity plan with clear recovery objectives and timelines

Answer: C) Conduct a thorough analysis of IT service continuity risks and impacts on business operations

Explanation: Conducting a thorough analysis of IT service continuity risks and impacts on business operations enables the organization to identify and mitigate risks, ensuring effective IT service continuity and business resilience.

Question 185

An organization is implementing ITIL 4 to improve its IT service management capabilities. The organization has a complex IT infrastructure with multiple IoT devices, networks, and integrations.

How can the organization ensure effective IT service management for IoT devices?

A) Implement an IoT service management framework that integrates with existing ITSM processes

B) Establish an IoT center of excellence to oversee IoT service management

C) Conduct a thorough analysis of IoT device dependencies and impacts on IT services

D) Develop a comprehensive IoT service catalog to showcase IoT services to stakeholders

Answer: A) Implement an IoT service management framework that integrates with existing ITSM processes

Explanation: Implementing an IoT service management framework that integrates with existing ITSM processes enables the organization to manage IoT devices effectively, ensuring seamless integration with existing IT services and processes.

Question 186

An IT service provider is experiencing issues with its IT service level management process, resulting in poor customer satisfaction. The organization has a large IT service portfolio with multiple stakeholders, vendors, and dependencies. How can the organization improve its IT service level management process to ensure effective IT service delivery?

A) Implement a service level management framework that accounts for service dependencies

B) Establish a service level agreement (SLA) management team to oversee SLA performance

C) Conduct a thorough analysis of customer expectations and service level requirements

D) Develop a comprehensive service level report to showcase SLA performance to stakeholders

Answer: C) Conduct a thorough analysis of customer expectations and service level requirements

Explanation: Conducting a thorough analysis of customer expectations and service level requirements enables the organization to develop effective SLAs that meet customer needs, improving customer satisfaction and loyalty.

Question 187

An organization is implementing ITIL 4 to improve its IT service management capabilities. The organization wants to optimize its ITSM processes for efficiency. Which of the following activities can help achieve ITSM efficiency?

A) Automating repetitive ITSM tasks and workflows

B) Implementing a comprehensive ITSM training program for staff

C) Conducting regular ITSM process audits and assessments

D) Developing a comprehensive ITSM dashboard for reporting and analytics

Answer: A) Automating repetitive ITSM tasks and workflows

Explanation: Automating repetitive ITSM tasks and workflows can help achieve ITSM efficiency by reducing manual effort, minimizing errors, and increasing productivity.

Q

Question 188

An IT service provider is experiencing issues with its ITSM process efficiency, resulting in delayed incident resolution and poor customer satisfaction. Which of the following activities can help improve ITSM process efficiency?

A) Implementing a lean ITSM approach to eliminate waste and optimize processes

B) Establishing a comprehensive ITSM knowledge management system

C) Conducting regular ITSM process reviews and retrospectives

D) Developing a comprehensive ITSM metrics and reporting framework

Answer: A) Implementing a lean ITSM approach to eliminate waste and optimize processes

Explanation: Implementing a lean ITSM approach can help improve ITSM process efficiency by identifying and eliminating waste, optimizing processes, and improving flow.

Question 189

Which of the following ITIL 4 central principles emphasizes the importance of understanding and meeting customer needs and expectations?

A) Focus on Value

B) Design for Experience

C) Collaborate and Promote Visibility

D) Think and Act Holistically

Answer: A) Focus on Value

Explanation: The ITIL 4 central principle "Focus on Value" emphasizes the importance of understanding and meeting customer needs and expectations, ensuring that IT services deliver value to customers and stakeholders.

Question 190

Which of the following ITIL 4 central principles encourages organizations to consider the end-to-end value stream and optimize IT services accordingly?

A) Think and Act Holistically

B) Collaborate and Promote Visibility

C) Keep it Simple and Practical

D) Optimize and Automate

Answer: A) Think and Act Holistically

Explanation: The ITIL 4 central principle "Think and Act Holistically" encourages organizations to consider the end-to-end value stream, understanding the interconnectedness of IT services and optimizing them to deliver value to customers and stakeholders.

Question 191

Which of the following ITIL 4 central principles emphasizes the importance of collaboration and communication across teams and departments to deliver effective IT services?

A) Collaborate and Promote Visibility

B) Think and Act Holistically

C) Focus on Value

D) Keep it Simple and Practical

Answer: A) Collaborate and Promote Visibility

Explanation: The ITIL 4 central principle "Collaborate and Promote Visibility" emphasizes the importance of collaboration and communication across teams and departments to deliver effective IT services, ensuring that everyone works together towards common goals.

Question 192

Which of the following ITIL 4 central principles encourages organizations to simplify and streamline their IT services and processes, eliminating unnecessary complexity?

A) Keep it Simple and Practical

B) Optimize and Automate

C) Think and Act Holistically

D) Focus on Value

Answer: A) Keep it Simple and Practical

Explanation: The ITIL 4 central principle "Keep it Simple and Practical" encourages organizations to simplify and streamline their IT services and processes, eliminating unnecessary complexity and ensuring that IT services are easy to use and manage.

Question 193

Which of the following ITIL 4 central principles emphasizes the importance of designing IT services that are easy to use, meet customer needs, and provide a positive experience?

A) Design for Experience

B) Focus on Value

C) Collaborate and Promote Visibility

D) Think and Act Holistically

Answer: A) Design for Experience

Explanation: The ITIL 4 central principle "Design for Experience" emphasizes the importance of designing IT services that are easy to use, meet customer needs, and provide a positive experience, ensuring that IT services are user-friendly and meet customer expectations.

Question 194

Which of the following ITIL 4 central principles encourages organizations to continually improve and iterate their IT services and processes, using feedback and data to drive improvements?

A) Optimize and Automate

B) Keep it Simple and Practical

C) Think and Act Holistically

D) Progress Iteratively with Feedback

Answer: D) Progress Iteratively with Feedback

Explanation: The ITIL 4 central principle "Progress Iteratively with Feedback" encourages organizations to continually improve and iterate their IT services and processes, using feedback and data to drive improvements, ensuring that IT services are continually aligned with customer needs and expectations.

QUESTION 195

Which ITIL 4 process is responsible for ensuring that IT services are delivered to agreed-upon quality and performance standards, and that service level agreements (SLAs) are met?

A) Service Level Management

B) Service Quality Management

C) Continual Service Improvement

D) Service Validation and Testing

Answer: A) Service Level Management

Explanation: Service Level Management is the ITIL 4 process responsible for ensuring that IT services are delivered to agreed-upon quality and performance standards, and that SLAs are met.

Question 196

Which ITIL 4 process is responsible for identifying, assessing, and mitigating risks to IT services, and for ensuring that IT services are resilient and can recover quickly from disruptions?

A) Information Security Management

B) IT Service Continuity Management

C) Risk Management

D) Problem Management

Answer: B) IT Service Continuity Management

Explanation: IT Service Continuity Management is the ITIL 4 process responsible for identifying, assessing, and mitigating risks to IT services, and for ensuring that IT services are resilient and can recover quickly from disruptions.

Question 197

Which of the following ITIL 4 best practices involves identifying and managing risks that could impact IT services, and implementing measures to mitigate or manage those risks?

A) Continual Improvement

B) Service Level Management

C) Risk Management

D) Capacity Management

Answer: C) Risk Management

Explanation: Risk Management is one of the 15 ITIL best practices, and it involves identifying and managing risks that could impact IT services, and implementing measures to mitigate or manage those risks.

Question 198

Which of the following ITIL 4 best practices involves ensuring that IT services are designed and delivered to meet the needs of customers and end-users, and that customer satisfaction is measured and improved?

A) Service Desk

B) Service Validation and Testing

C) Service Design

D) Continual Service Improvement

Answer: C) Service Design

Explanation: Service Design is one of the 15 ITIL best practices, and it involves ensuring that IT services are designed and delivered to meet the needs of customers and end-users, and that customer satisfaction is measured and improved.

Question 199

Which stage of the ITIL 4 Service Value Chain involves designing and creating IT services to meet customer needs and expectations?

A) Engage

B) Design and Obtain/Build

C) Obtain/Build

D) Deliver and Support

Answer: B) Design and Obtain/Build

Explanation: The Design and Obtain/Build stage of the ITIL 4 Service Value Chain involves designing and creating IT services to meet customer needs and expectations, including the design of service components, processes, and interfaces.

Question 200

Which stage of the ITIL 4 Service Value Chain involves delivering and supporting IT services to customers, including service desk, incident management, and problem management?

A) Engage

B) Design and Obtain/Build

C) Deliver and Support

D) Obtain/Build

Answer: C) Deliver and Support

Explanation: The Deliver and Support stage of the ITIL 4 Service Value Chain involves delivering and supporting IT services to customers, including service desk, incident management, problem management, and other support activities to ensure that services are delivered to agreed-upon quality and performance standards.

PRACTICE TEST - 6

Question 201

Which Design and Transition activity involves creating a detailed plan for the transition of a new or changed IT service into production, including timelines, resources, and stakeholders?

A) Service Design

B) Service Transition Planning

C) Change Management

D) Release Management

Answer: B) Service Transition Planning

Explanation: Service Transition Planning is a Design and Transition activity that involves creating a detailed plan for the transition of a new or changed IT service into production, including timelines, resources, and stakeholders.

Question 202

Which Design and Transition activity involves building, testing, and deploying IT service components, including infrastructure, applications, and data?

A) Service Design

B) Service Build

C) Release Management

D) Deployment Management

Answer: B) Service Build

Explanation: Service Build is a Design and Transition activity that involves building, testing, and deploying IT service components, including infrastructure, applications, and data, to ensure that they are properly configured and meet the required specifications.

Question 203

Which Design and Transition activity involves evaluating and ensuring that IT services meet agreed-upon requirements and specifications before they are released into production?

A) Service Validation

B) Service Testing

C) Service Quality Assurance

D) Service Acceptance

Answer: A) Service Validation

Explanation: Service Validation is a Design and Transition activity that involves evaluating and ensuring that IT services meet agreed-upon requirements and specifications before they are released into production, to ensure that they are fit for purpose and meet customer needs.

Question 204

Which Design and Transition activity involves managing the movement of releases through the service lifecycle, from development to deployment, to ensure that changes are properly assessed, approved, and implemented?

A) Release Management

B) Change Management

C) Service Build

D) Deployment Management

Answer: A) Release Management

Explanation: Release Management is a Design and Transition activity that involves managing the movement of releases through the service lifecycle, from development to deployment, to ensure that changes are properly assessed, approved, and implemented, and that IT services are delivered to agreed-upon quality and performance standards.

Question 205

Which Design and Transition activity involves identifying, assessing, and mitigating risks associated with the transition of new or changed IT services into production?

A) Service Risk Management

B) Change Management

C) Service Validation

D) Service Transition Planning

Answer: A) Service Risk Management

Explanation: Service Risk Management is a Design and Transition activity that involves identifying, assessing, and mitigating risks associated with the transition of new or changed IT services into production, to ensure that potential impacts on IT services are minimized.

Question 206

Which Design and Transition activity involves ensuring that IT services are properly configured, tested, and validated before they are released into production, to ensure that they meet agreed-upon requirements and specifications?

A) Service Testing

B) Service Validation

C) Service Build

D) Deployment Management

Answer: B) Service Validation

Explanation: Service Validation is a Design and Transition activity that involves ensuring that IT services are properly configured, tested, and validated before they are released into production, to ensure that they meet agreed-upon requirements and specifications, and are fit for purpose.

Question 207

Which Deliver and Support activity involves restoring normal IT service operation as quickly as possible following an unplanned interruption or disruption?

A) Incident Management

B) Problem Management

C) Service Request Management

D) Service Desk

Answer: A) Incident Management

Explanation: Incident Management is a Deliver and Support activity that involves restoring normal IT service operation as quickly as possible following an unplanned interruption or disruption, to minimize the impact on business operations.

Question 208

Which Deliver and Support activity involves identifying and resolving the root cause of incidents to prevent future occurrences?

A) Incident Management

B) Problem Management

C) Service Request Management

D) Continual Service Improvement

Answer: B) Problem Management

Explanation: Problem Management is a Deliver and Support activity that involves identifying and resolving the root cause of incidents to prevent future occurrences, to improve the overall quality and reliability of IT services.

Question 209

What is the primary goal of the Service Desk function in the Deliver and Support activity of the ITIL 4 Service Value Chain?

A) To resolve all incidents and requests without escalation

B) To provide a single point of contact for customers and end-users

C) To manage and coordinate all IT service management processes

D) To monitor and control all IT services and infrastructure

Answer: B) To provide a single point of contact for customers and end-users

Explanation: The primary goal of the Service Desk function is to provide a single point of contact for customers and end-users, to ensure that all their inquiries, requests, and incidents are properly logged, tracked, and resolved in a timely and efficient manner.

Question 210

Which Deliver and Support activity involves managing and fulfilling customer and end-user requests for new or changed IT services, such as password resets, software installations, or access requests?

A) Service Request Management

B) Incident Management

C) Problem Management

D) Change Management

Answer: A) Service Request Management

Explanation: Service Request Management is the Deliver and Support activity that involves managing and fulfilling customer and end-user requests for new or changed IT services, such as password resets, software installations, or access requests, to ensure that customers and end-users receive the IT services they need to perform their jobs.

Question 211

What is the primary objective of the Continual Service Improvement (CSI) activity in the Deliver and Support stage of the ITIL 4 Service Value Chain?

A) To identify and implement service improvements to increase customer satisfaction

B) To manage and resolve incidents and requests

C) To monitor and control IT services and infrastructure

D) To design and transition new or changed IT services

Answer: A) To identify and implement service improvements to increase customer satisfaction

Explanation: The primary objective of the Continual Service Improvement (CSI) activity is to identify and implement service improvements to increase customer satisfaction, by identifying opportunities for improvement, analyzing data, and implementing changes to improve the quality and value of IT services.

Question 212

Which Deliver and Support activity involves monitoring and controlling IT services and infrastructure to ensure that they are operating within agreed-upon parameters and that incidents are quickly identified and resolved?

A) Technical Management

B) Service Desk

C) IT Service Continuity Management

D) Monitoring and Control

Answer: D) Monitoring and Control

Explanation: Monitoring and Control is the Deliver and Support activity that involves monitoring and controlling IT services and infrastructure to ensure that they are operating within agreed-upon parameters and that incidents are quickly identified and resolved, to ensure that IT services are delivered to agreed-upon quality and performance standards.

Question 213

Which of the following is an example of a Service Value Stream in ITIL 4?

A) Incident Management process

B) Change Management process

C) End-to-end flow of activities to deliver a specific IT service to customers

D) IT service desk function

Answer: C) End-to-end flow of activities to deliver a specific IT service to customers

Explanation: A Service Value Stream is an end-to-end flow of activities that creates and delivers a specific IT service to customers, from demand to value realization. It involves multiple processes and activities working together to deliver value to customers.

Question 214

What is the primary benefit of defining and managing Service Value Streams in ITIL 4?

A) Improved incident resolution times

B) Increased efficiency of IT processes

C) Enhanced customer experience and value realization

D) Better alignment of IT services with business strategy

Answer: C) Enhanced customer experience and value realization

Explanation: The primary benefit of defining and managing Service Value Streams is to enhance customer experience and value realization, by ensuring that IT services are delivered in a way that meets customer needs and expectations, and that value is created and realized throughout the service lifecycle.

Question 215

Which of the following is a key characteristic of a Service Value Stream in ITIL 4?

A) Focus on a single IT process or activity

B) End-to-end flow of activities across multiple processes

C) Emphasis on technical metrics and performance

D) Limited to internal IT stakeholders only

Answer: B) End-to-end flow of activities across multiple processes

Explanation: A Service Value Stream is characterized by an end-to-end flow of activities across multiple processes, from demand to value realization, to deliver a specific IT service to customers.

Question 216

What is the primary purpose of defining and managing Service Value Streams in ITIL 4?

A) To optimize individual IT processes and activities

B) To improve communication and collaboration between IT teams

C) To deliver value to customers and stakeholders through IT services

D) To reduce IT costs and improve efficiency

Answer: C) To deliver value to customers and stakeholders through IT services

Explanation: The primary purpose of defining and managing Service Value Streams is to deliver value to customers and stakeholders through IT services, by ensuring that IT services are designed, delivered, and supported in a way that meets customer needs and expectations.

Question 217

Which of the following best describes the concept of "Demand" in the context of Service Value Streams in ITIL 4?

A) Customer requests for IT services

B) Business requirements for IT services

C) The triggering of a service request or incident

D) The start of the service development lifecycle

Answer: A) Customer requests for IT services

Explanation: In the context of Service Value Streams, "Demand" refers to customer requests for IT services, which triggers the service value chain and the flow of activities to deliver value to customers.

Question 218

What is the primary benefit of using the "Engage" activity in a Service Value Stream in ITIL 4?

A) To design and develop IT services

B) To transition IT services into production

C) To ensure customer and stakeholder engagement and feedback

D) To monitor and control IT services

Answer: C) To ensure customer and stakeholder engagement and feedback

Explanation: The primary benefit of using the "Engage" activity in a Service Value Stream is to ensure customer and stakeholder engagement and feedback, to understand their needs and expectations and to ensure that the IT service meets their requirements.

Question 219

Which of the following is a key output of the "Design and Obtain/Build" activity in a Service Value Stream in ITIL 4?

A) A service request or incident resolution

B) A designed and built IT service or component

C) A transition plan for moving a service into production

D) A monitoring and control plan for an IT service

Answer: B) A designed and built IT service or component

Explanation: The "Design and Obtain/Build" activity in a Service Value Stream is responsible for designing and building IT services or components, to meet customer and business requirements.

Question 220

What is the primary purpose of the "Obtain/Build" component of the "Design and Obtain/Build" activity in a Service Value Stream in ITIL 4?

A) To design IT services and components

B) To procure or build IT services and components

C) To test and validate IT services and components

D) To transition IT services and components into production

Answer: B) To procure or build IT services and components

Explanation: The "Obtain/Build" component of the "Design and Obtain/Build" activity is responsible for procuring or building IT services and components, to ensure that they are available for use in the IT service.

QUESTION 221

Which of the following activities in a Service Value Stream is responsible for ensuring that IT services are delivered and supported according to agreed-upon requirements and specifications?

A) Engage

B) Design and Obtain/Build

C) Transition

D) Obtain/Build and Deliver and Support

Answer: D) Obtain/Build and Deliver and Support

Explanation: The "Obtain/Build" and "Deliver and Support" activities in a Service Value Stream are responsible for ensuring that IT services are delivered and supported according to agreed-upon requirements and specifications.

Question 222

What is the primary benefit of using the "Deliver and Support" activity in a Service Value Stream in ITIL 4?

A) To design and develop IT services

B) To transition IT services into production

C) To ensure ongoing delivery and support of IT services

D) To monitor and control IT services

Answer: C) To ensure ongoing delivery and support of IT services

Explanation: The primary benefit of using the "Deliver and Support" activity in a Service Value Stream is to ensure ongoing delivery and support of IT services, to ensure that they continue to meet customer and business requirements."

Question 223

Which of the following is a key characteristic of the "Deliver and Support" activity in a Service Value Stream in ITIL 4?

A) Focus on designing and building IT services

B) Emphasis on transitioning IT services into production

C) Ongoing delivery and support of IT services to customers

D) Limited to internal IT stakeholders only

Answer: C) Ongoing delivery and support of IT services to customers

Explanation: The "Deliver and Support" activity in a Service Value Stream is characterized by an ongoing delivery and support of IT services to customers, to ensure that they continue to meet customer and business requirements.

Question 224

What is the primary purpose of the "Realize Value" activity in a Service Value Stream in ITIL 4?

A) To design and develop IT services

B) To transition IT services into production

C) To ensure ongoing delivery and support of IT services

D) To ensure that value is realized from IT services by customers

Answer: D) To ensure that value is realized from IT services by customers

Explanation: The primary purpose of the "Realize Value" activity in a Service Value Stream is to ensure that value is realized from IT services by customers, by ensuring that the services meet customer needs and expectations, and that the benefits of the services are achieved.

Question 225

Which of the following activities in a Service Value Stream is responsible for ensuring that the value of IT services is measured and reported to stakeholders?

A) Engage

B) Design and Obtain/Build

C) Deliver and Support

D) Realize Value

Answer: D) Realize Value

Explanation: The "Realize Value" activity in a Service Value Stream is responsible for ensuring that the value of IT services is measured and reported to stakeholders, to ensure that the benefits of the services are achieved and that value is realized.

Question 226

What is the primary benefit of using the "Realize Value" activity in a Service Value Stream in ITIL 4?

A) Improved efficiency of IT processes

B) Enhanced customer satisfaction

C) Increased value realization from IT services

D) Better alignment of IT services with business strategy

Answer: C) Increased value realization from IT services

Explanation: The primary benefit of using the "Realize Value" activity in a Service Value Stream is to increase value realization from IT services, by ensuring that the benefits of the services are achieved and that value is realized by customers and stakeholders.

Question 227

Which of the following is a key output of the "Realize Value" activity in a Service Value Stream in ITIL 4?

A) A designed and built IT service

B) A transition plan for moving a service into production

C) A report on the value realized from an IT service

D) A service request or incident resolution

Answer: C) A report on the value realized from an IT service

Explanation: The "Realize Value" activity in a Service Value Stream is responsible for producing a report on the value realized from an IT service, to ensure that stakeholders understand the benefits and value achieved from the service.

Question 228

What is the primary purpose of the "Improve and Learn" activity in a Service Value Stream in ITIL 4?

A) To design and develop IT services

B) To transition IT services into production

C) To ensure ongoing delivery and support of IT services

D) To identify and implement improvements to IT services and processes

Answer: D) To identify and implement improvements to IT services and processes

Explanation: The primary purpose of the "Improve and Learn" activity in a Service Value Stream is to identify and implement improvements to IT services and processes, to ensure that they remain effective and efficient over time.

Question 229

Which of the following activities in a Service Value Stream is responsible for identifying and implementing improvements to IT services and processes?

A) Engage

B) Design and Obtain/Build

C) Deliver and Support

D) Improve and Learn

Answer: D) Improve and Learn

Explanation: The "Improve and Learn" activity in a Service Value Stream is responsible for identifying and implementing improvements to IT services and processes, to ensure that they remain effective and efficient over time.

Question 230

What is the primary benefit of using the "Improve and Learn" activity in a Service Value Stream in ITIL 4?

A) Improved efficiency of IT processes

B) Enhanced customer satisfaction

C) Increased value realization from IT services

D) Continuous improvement and learning culture

Answer: D) Continuous improvement and learning culture

Explanation: The primary benefit of using the "Improve and Learn" activity in a Service Value Stream is to create a continuous improvement and learning culture, where IT services and processes are regularly reviewed and improved to ensure they remain effective and efficient.

Question 231

Which of the following is a key characteristic of the "Improve and Learn" activity in a Service Value Stream in ITIL 4?

A) Focus on designing and building IT services

B) Emphasis on transitioning IT services into production

C) Continuous improvement and learning culture

D) Limited to internal IT stakeholders only

Answer: C) Continuous improvement and learning culture

Explanation: The "Improve and Learn" activity in a Service Value Stream is characterized by a continuous improvement and learning culture, where IT services and processes are regularly reviewed and improved to ensure they remain effective and efficient.

Question 232

What is the primary purpose of the "Improve and Learn" activity in relation to the Service Value System in ITIL 4?

A) To design and develop IT services

B) To manage and improve the Service Value System

C) To ensure ongoing delivery and support of IT services

D) To measure and report on IT service performance

Answer: B) To manage and improve the Service Value System

Explanation: The primary purpose of the "Improve and Learn" activity is to manage and improve the Service Value System, by identifying and implementing improvements to IT services and processes, and ensuring that the Service Value System remains effective and efficient.

Question 233

Which of the following activities in a Service Value Stream is responsible for ensuring that IT services are aligned with changing business needs?

A) Engage

B) Design and Obtain/Build

C) Deliver and Support

D) Improve and Learn

Answer: D) Improve and Learn

Explanation: The "Improve and Learn" activity in a Service Value Stream is responsible for ensuring that IT services are aligned with changing business needs, by regularly reviewing and improving IT services and processes to ensure they remain effective and efficient.

Question 234

What is the primary benefit of using the "Improve and Learn" activity to review and improve IT services and processes in a Service Value Stream?

A) Improved efficiency of IT processes

B) Enhanced customer satisfaction

C) Increased value realization from IT services

D) Ability to adapt to changing business needs

Answer: D) Ability to adapt to changing business needs

Explanation: The primary benefit of using the "Improve and Learn" activity to review and improve IT services and processes is the ability to adapt to changing business needs, by ensuring that IT services remain aligned with business objectives and requirements.

Question 235

Which of the following factors influences technology in IT service management, according to ITIL 4?

A) Business requirements and objectives

B) Customer needs and expectations

C) Technology advancements and innovations

D) All of the above

Answer: D) All of the above

Explanation: According to ITIL 4, several factors influence technology in IT service management, including business requirements and objectives, customer needs and expectations, and technology advancements and innovations.

Question 236

What is the primary impact of technological advancements on IT service management, according to ITIL 4?

A) Increased complexity and costs

B) Improved efficiency and effectiveness

C) Enhanced customer experience and satisfaction

D) All of the above

Answer: D) All of the above

Explanation: According to ITIL 4, technological advancements can have several impacts on IT service management, including increased complexity and costs, improved efficiency and effectiveness, and enhanced customer experience and satisfaction.

Question 237

Which of the following cloud computing deployment models is characterized by a single organization using a cloud environment for its own use, according to ITIL 4?

A) Public Cloud

B) Private Cloud

C) Hybrid Cloud

D) Community Cloud

Answer: B) Private Cloud

Explanation: According to ITIL 4, a private cloud is a cloud computing deployment model where a single organization uses a cloud environment for its own use, providing greater control and security.

Question 238

What is the primary benefit of using a hybrid cloud deployment model, according to ITIL 4?

A) Increased security and control

B) Improved scalability and flexibility

C) Enhanced cost savings and efficiency

D) Better alignment with business requirements

Answer: B) Improved scalability and flexibility

Explanation: According to ITIL 4, the primary benefit of using a hybrid cloud deployment model is improved scalability and flexibility, as it allows organizations to take advantage of the strengths of both public and private clouds.

Question 239

Which of the following cloud computing service models provides customers with a complete platform for developing, running, and managing applications, according to ITIL 4?

A) Infrastructure as a Service (IaaS)

B) Platform as a Service (PaaS)

C) Software as a Service (SaaS)

D) Desktop as a Service (DaaS)

Answer: B) Platform as a Service (PaaS)

Explanation: According to ITIL 4, Platform as a Service (PaaS) provides customers with a complete platform for developing, running, and managing applications, including tools, libraries, and infrastructure.

Question 240

What is the primary benefit of using cloud computing in IT service management, according to ITIL 4?

A) Improved security and compliance

B) Increased cost savings and efficiency

C) Enhanced scalability and flexibility

D) Better alignment with business requirements

Answer: C) Enhanced scalability and flexibility

Explanation: According to ITIL 4, the primary benefit of using cloud computing in IT service management is enhanced scalability and flexibility, as cloud computing allows organizations to quickly scale up or down to meet changing business needs.

End Note

As you reach the final pages of "ITIL 4 Foundation Exam Insights: Q & A with Explanations," I extend my warmest congratulations on your steadfast commitment to mastering the ITIL 4 Foundation certification. Your dedication to navigating through the numerous questions, insightful answers, and thorough explanations in this book is a testament to your ambition and perseverance in the realm of IT service management.

Remember, achieving success in the ITIL 4 Foundation exam is not just about passing a test; it represents a deeper understanding of IT service management principles and their practical application in enhancing service delivery and organizational efficiency. Whether you are on the brink of taking the ITIL 4 Foundation exam or using this book to fine-tune your ITSM expertise, the knowledge you've acquired will be a valuable asset in your professional journey.

Your commitment to continuous learning and professional development is truly admirable. As you move forward, I encourage you to apply the insights and skills gained from "ITIL 4 Foundation Exam Insights" to drive excellence in your IT service management practices. May this book continue to be a reliable guide, helping you navigate the evolving landscape of ITSM with confidence and success. Best wishes as you continue to grow and excel in your career!

***Please note that the example questions included in "ITIL 4 Foundation Exam Insights: Q & A with Explanations" are designed for illustrative purposes only and may not represent the actual questions on the ITIL 4 Foundation exam. Their primary goal is to offer you a sense of the question format and to provide practice in applying your ITIL knowledge effectively.

To ensure comprehensive exam preparation, it is essential to consult the official ITIL 4 resources and study materials. These will provide the most accurate and up-to-date information needed to succeed on the exam. This book aims to complement your study efforts by reinforcing your understanding and helping you apply ITIL principles in a practical context.

Thank you for choosing this guide as part of your study journey. May it serve as a valuable tool in your preparation and contribute to your success in achieving ITIL 4 Foundation certification. Best of luck as you continue to advance your expertise in IT service management!

***WE APOLOGIZE FOR ANY inadvertent repetition of questions you may encounter in "ITIL 4 Foundation Exam Insights: Q & A with Explanations." Please be assured that any repeated questions were not intentional. If you notice any such occurrences, we appreciate your understanding and patience.

Our primary goal is to offer you a rich and diverse range of content to enhance your learning experience and preparation. We are committed to supporting you in your journey toward ITIL 4 Foundation certification and aim to provide you with valuable insights and practical knowledge.

Thank you for your understanding and for choosing this book as part of your study resources. We wish you the best of luck in your exam preparation and future career in IT service management.

Also by SUJAN

PMP Practice Test Navigator: Nailing the Exam
PMP Success: Ultimate Exam Questions & Answers
PMP Exam Companion
CAPM Success Blueprint
AgileQuest: Unlocking PMI-ACP Success
PMI-RMP Exam Companion
PMI-PBA Exam Success :A Practical Guide to Ace Business Analysis Questions
CAPM Success Path : MCQs and Explanations for Prep Excellence
CAPM Q-Connect
CAPM Exam Insights: Q&A with Explanations
PMI-ACP Success Path: Q&A with Explanations
PMI-ACP Exam Insights: Q&A with Explanations
PMI-PgMP Exam Insights: Q&A with Explanations
PMI-SP Success Blueprint: Q&A with Explanations
PMI-RMP Success Blueprint :Q&A with Explanations
PfMP Exam Companion: Q&A with Explanations
PMP Exam Insights: Q&A with Explanations
PMI-RMP Exam Insights: Q&A with Explanations
PMI-PgMP Exam Companion: Q&A with Explanations
CAPM Essentials: Expert Q&A with Detailed Explanations
PMI-PgMP Exam Excellence: Q&A with In-Depth Explanations
PMI-PgMP Exam Navigator: Expert Q&A with Detailed Explanations
PMI-PgMP Success Blueprint: Q&A with Explanations

PMI-PgMP SURE SUCCESS: Q&A with Explanations
CAPM SURE SUCCESS: Expert Q&A with Detailed Explanations
PMI-RMP Sure Success : Q&A with Explanations
PMI-ACP Sure Success: Q&A with Explanations
PfMP Exam Insights : Q&A with Explanations
AWS Certified Solutions Architect Associate Exam Insights : Q&A with Explanations
ISTQB Advanced Level Technical Test Analyst- Exam Insights: Q&A with Explanations
ITIL 4 Foundation Exam Insights: Q & A with Explanations